STRINDBERG

THE ORIGIN OF PSYCHOLOGY IN MODERN DRAMA

STRINDBERG

THE ORIGIN OF PSYCHOLOGY IN MODERN DRAMA

by FRANKLIN S. KLAF, M.D.

Introduction by John Gassner

THE CITADEL PRESS   NEW YORK

FIRST EDITION

Copyright © 1963 by Franklin S. Klaf

Library of Congress Catalogue Card No. *63-21206*

FRONTISPIECE BY ANNA MARIE MAGAGNA

CONTENTS

INTRODUCTION

STRINDBERG: PEARL *and* OYSTER

by JOHN GASSNER

What I like most about Dr. Franklin Klaf's book is its interest in *health,* not disease. Although he is chiefly concerned with the nature and etiology of Strindberg's mental disturbance, Dr. Klaf makes it clear that Strindberg's immense literary labors kept him from permanently crossing the tenuous border between sanity and insanity, facilitated rapid, if incomplete, recovery when he did overstep, and preserved him as a literary master when simple recovery might have produced merely a subdued and delicately balanced discharged patient. "Genius plus application to creative work" might prove a good formula for psychotherapy if only one knew how to provide genius and make sure that it is creatively employed.

Dr. Klaf's formidable collection of data concerning the imbalance of Strindberg's psyche will be interesting as a case history to those who are professionally interested in case histories. I cannot imagine it to be otherwise, although I must own up to a personal distaste for words like "insanity" and "schizophrenia" when applied to men of productive talent. But the struggle for health in Strindberg's case possesses a fascination for the lay reader that ranges far beyond the psychiatric clinic and the psychoanalyst's couch. The mother fixation that flared up periodically

in Strindberg's life, the accompanying exaggerated expectations and disappointments of his matrimonial ventures,
the paranoid delusions of grandeur that made an alchemist
of him and the delusions of persecution that bereft him
of peace and perspective in personal relations—these and
other morbid manifestations can become decidedly tiresome as clinical phenomena. Only in so far as he made
distinguished fiction, drama, and literary autobiography
with them can they be considered more than tolerable to
any but clinically interested readers.

In appreciating Strindberg the *artist* even his admirers
have sometimes evinced irritation with Strindberg the
neurotic, as when the British critic Desmond MacCarthy
referred to the playwright's well-aired domestic conflicts
as "the sorrows of a henpecked bluebeard." Even when
the two Strindbergs, the genius and the psychopath, appear to be the same individual, we prefer to divorce the
infirm creator from his properly crystallized creation;
we like to separate the pearl from the sick oyster. In the
case of Strindberg, it is gratifying to observe his artistic
victories over disease and exhilarating to find him transforming common enough morbidity into uncommonly absorbing drama. His symptoms, as Dr. Klaf relates them, are
the classical ones in psychopathology, but we are ultimately
interested in those powers of resilience, projection, and
transformation observable in his writing that distinguished
Strindberg from other patients and made him the father
of modern psychological drama. He had *illness* in common
with them, but they did not have *genius* in common with
him; and in his possession and exercise of genius lay, in
fact, his essential *health*.

Dr. Klaf perceives all this and presents it with professional authority. He therefore follows Strindberg into the
world of his art and leads us into it appreciatively instead

of allowing himself to be mired in the minutiae of neurosis and psychosis. Although his excursions into literary and dramatic criticism are necessarily limited, he makes it abundantly evident that it is there, in Strindberg's works, that we shall find what is unique about his subject. In this sense it is possible to say that Dr. Klaf studies the patient's health while recording his disease. What this consists of, aside from the end-result of social acceptance as a distinguished writer, is an endowment also possessed by "normal" men who became distinguished authors, although it was probably less hard-won in their case. It could be said of Strindberg that in possessing powers of acute sensibility, vivid externalization, vigorous projection, and keen perception he was like other good writers, only *more so*. If this had not been the case, indeed, his dramatic work could not have been superior, as it indisputably is, to the work of all but possibly two or three modern dramatists.

Insight, into himself and into others, is an especially significant attribute of his art, and therefore of his health, too. (Disease may have, of course, sharpened insight even while subverting it in some of his writings and producing the abnormal suspicions and delusions of persecution from which he suffered to various degrees virtually throughout his life.) He manifests this insight early in his work, and it even increases and deepens with experience. This is, of course, what the mentally disturbed lack and what it is hoped therapy will enable them to attain at least so far as their illness is concerned. If Strindberg lost insight or perspective from time to time, his recovery was usually swift and was followed by renewed creativity. He had a major psychotic episode in 1897, but it is remarkable how after leaving his sanatorium (and leaving it by no means completely liberated from tensions and delusions) he was able to produce an entire series of obective historical dramas such as "Gustav Vasa" and "Gustav Adolf" along with fantasies of the order of "To Damascus" in which deep-seated guilt feelings are objectified and the troubled spirit is temporarily pacified.

Many who appear to possess insights are unable to articulate them. In this respect Strindberg could not be faulted even at the first great stage of his career in the late 1880's, when he created naturalistic psychological drama, and his growing confidence in his craftsmanship enabled him within a decade to undertake deeper probings than any previously attempted that affected dramatic form itself. The deeper he mined the human psyche the more he resorted to complex and original techniques with which to present the apparitions of subjective experience. Only a writer confident of mastery of the dramatic medium would have dared to depart, not once by accident but many times by design, from the norms of imitation and stage representation as Strindberg did in moving from realistic to expressionist drama—from the dramatic style of "The Father" or "Miss Julie," for example, to that of "A Dream Play" and "The Ghost Sonata."

Strindberg penetrated with his expressionist plays into the very recesses of the Unconscious or the dream so usefully explored in twentieth-century metapsychology and psychopathology. And although he had but recently recovered from his psychotic crisis he was completely aware of what he was doing when he wrote his series of nonnaturalistic dramas beginning with the first two parts of "To Damascus" in 1898. His understanding of means and ends is especially evident in his celebrated preface to "A Dream Play," in which he describes his use of dream technique in that play and in "To Damascus." He tells his readers that he has resorted to "the detached and disunited—although apparently logical—form of dreams." In "A Dream Play" time and space have no reality and anything is possible and will seem probable: "On a flimsy foundation of actual happenings, imagination spins, and weaves in new patterns: an intermingling of remembrances, experiences, whims, fancies, ideas, fantastic absurdities and improvisations, and original inventions of the mind." And in the play dominated by the dreamer, "the personalities split, take on duality, multiply, vanish, intensify, diffuse and disperse, and are brought into focus." (Arvid Paulson's translation.)

Intention and execution matching, Strindberg not only introduced a new subject matter in giving primacy to psychological conflicts but created a new dramatic form. He fathered not only modern psychological drama but modern expressionist style, which has had a constant direct and indirect effect on the theatre since the end of the nineteenth century second only to that of dramatic realism.

When in an earlier period, during the late 1880's, Strindberg favored strict realism in his plays as a dedicated "naturalist" he was no less aware of intent and procedure than when he became an "expressionist," as may be particularly observed in his Preface to "Miss Julie." In fine, he had a way of crystalizing experience and emotion as "form," which was nothing less than an uncommon aptitude for knowing what he was doing in art even if he had a considerably less reliable aptitude for knowing what he was doing in life. He had "a will to form," one might say, and a concomitant "will to objectivity" which is particularly apparent in his confessional autobiographies from "The Son of a Servant" in 1886 to "Inferno" in 1897. And here again we may observe health or, as Bernard Shaw put it, "the sanity of art" supervening therapeutically upon disease, for nothing is so outer-directed and related to what is called "the reality principle" than conscious creativity. Dramatic writing is an especially exacting discipline. However unreasonable Strindberg's attraction-repulsion relationship with the women in his life and the reflection of the duel of the sexes in his literary work, he mastered a large portion of his inner disorder with his mastery of dramatic form. If this had not been the case, we might have known Strindberg as a magisterial psychopath but hardly as a master playwright.

Ego-centered to a greater degree than most men, but less blinded by concern with his ego than minor artists whose narcissism dooms them to be forever "minor," Strindberg could look over the fence of his egotism and see "other people," especially the women who were the antagonists in his plays and books. He could create characters instead of limiting himself to inquisitions and disquisitions, or to a dialectic of the mind, in dealing with the duel of the sexes. Consequently, too, his insights carried conviction, penetrating as they did into life—that is, into people as they are apt to be in their complexity and contradictoriness. Few playwrights have been as concerned with the tangle of causation, as if Strindberg had been heedful of the Viennese psychoanalyst Robert Wälder's later formulation of a "law of multiple motivation." Strindberg made much the same formulation in his remarkable Preface to "Miss Julie," in which he wrote that "A happening in life—and this is a fairly recent discovery!—is generally brought by a whole series of more or less deep-lying motives," and added, "I commend myself for the introduction of this multiplicity of motives." (Paulson translation.) Strindberg was one of those nineteenth-century observers, mostly poets, playwrights and novelists, who contributed subtleties of well-nigh diabolic perception to European romanticism and realism alike. He belonged to the company of Kleist, Novalis, Stendhal, Dostoevsky, and Nietzsche among others.

Had Dr. Klaf been so minded or so lavish with space as to provide a close analysis of some of Strindberg's best known dramas, he could easily have provided evidence of impressive artistic balance in Strindberg's works even when he presented literary surrogates of himself as victims of feminine parasitism and guile. In the first of his dramatic masterpieces," "The Father," for example, Strindberg shows his hero the Captain inviting defeat by his wife with his own flaws of characters, and he makes Laura, the husband-destroying Clytemnestra of the play, considerate to nearly everybody but the Captain, her would-be master. In the sex-duel central to "The Father," the Captain is no match for his wife, despite his superior intelligence, because he is insecure in his masculinity and parenthood, while Laura pushes her conflict with him to an extreme of destructiveness beyond her original intention and will. Villainess she may be, as well as representative of Strindberg's paranoid conception of women created in the image of his first wife, Siri von Essen, but it is essentially her husband's masculine self-assertiveness that arouses her compulsive, irrational enmity.

Strindberg, although greatly perturbed by the course of his first marriage while writing "The Father" in 1887, keeps antagonists in balance. There is no villainy or melodrama in the play in spite of the extreme violence of the interior and exterior action; there is only the action of characters driven to destruction and self-destruction by psychic forces Strindberg associated with a universal conflict between male and female. In other plays, too, such as "The Creditor," "The Link (or "The Bond"), and "The Dance of Death," Strindberg's husbands are not innocent martyrs, and individuals of both sexes are driven by impulses beyond reason and control. With that kind of treatment of character-motivated action Strindberg served reality, produced art, and created psychological drama all at the same time instead of simply projecting a psychosis or a series of psychotic reactions. I do not say that Strindberg was ever a happy man for long, but I believe it would be hard to find better examples of the transcendence as well as utilization of mental suffering in literary history.

Strindberg, we know, also went beyond individual psychology in his work and adopted the still wider perspectives of "social drama." He related domestic conflict to the social factors reflected and represented by the turn-of-the-century feminism and the rise of the so-called New Woman. He observed the growth of feminine domination of society in modern times. Like D. H. Lawrence decades later, he viewed sexual conflict as a special struggle for power. Conflicts between the upper and lower classes also came under his observation, and were both actually and symbolically represented in his writings. In "Miss Julie," for example, the antagonists of the sex duel are a valet and a countess who exemplify characteristic differences of class as well as of sex. Strindberg, indeed, found a parallel to the "war of the sexes" in the "class war," to which European literature became increasingly attentive after the revolutions of 1830 and 1848. Strindberg projected this conflict not only in his naturalistic plays but even in his expressionist fancies, as in the contrast he draws between the worlds of the rich and the poor in "A Dream Play" and in the vampire character of a household Cook in "The Ghost Sonata" who drains the strength out of her master's food. There is an *outside* world in Strindberg's consciousness, no matter how distorted it happens to be in certain periods of his life, and this is especially evident in his fiction and in his noteworthy series of historical plays.

So we come, I repeat, to the ineluctable conclusion that it is the *sanity* of art, not its insanity, that is exemplified in the career of Strindberg; its order, not disorder; its relatedness to reality, not evasion of reality; and the artist's mastery of chaotic tension, not a psychotic submission to it. The final result is integration, not disintegration. The fragments of a frequently exploded life are reassembled in Strindberg's art, conflict is momentarily stilled in the very process of being revealed, and a temporary reconciliation with existence is achieved even in the act of showing life to be as intolerable and illusory as it is in "A Dream Play." These are the paradoxes of creativity and among major modern writers will be found few who exemplified them so conspicuously and persistently as Strindberg did. More than anything else, this is what constitutes the modernity of the most "modern" of the theatre's writers, this dramatist of modern man's division and alienation.

Dr. Klaf's chronicle of Strindberg's struggle for mental health, lapses, and recoveries, pertains to the base upon which Strindberg erected works of recognition, projection, and transcendence besides which clinical facts alone must appear routine no matter how accurate and relevant. Dr. Klaf himself, and this is greatly to his credit, wants us to turn from the disease to the frequently won and precariously held sanity of the modern master. (I wish only that he had been more disposed than he is in the last chapter to do justice to the dramatic labors of the latter-day O'Neill.) Dr. Klaf does not gloss over the presence of neurosis and psychosis in his subject, but he knows that the creative power of the artist, the basis of his social value and distinction, lies in the deepest recesses of his personality. He could have said with Lionel Trilling that the one part of the artist that is healthy is "that which gives him the power to conceive, to plan, to work, and to bring his work to a conclusion." And he realizes that, like other major artists, Strindberg (as John Keats would have put it) was more than a dreaming thing and a fever of himself.

PREFACE

Contemporary dramatic literature, with its soul-searching agonies, owes more to the influence of the tormented Swedish playwright August Strindberg than to any other writer. Eugene O'Neill, Sean O'Casey, and Tennessee Williams have paid tribute to Strindberg as their predecessor and teacher, O'Casey lionizing him as "The Greatest of Them All." O'Neill acknowledged his debt in a letter to the Nobel Prize Committee—"It was reading his plays when I first started to write in the winter of 1913-1914 that, above all else, first gave me the vision of what modern drama could be—Strindberg is the greatest genius of all modern dramatists." Williams' portrayals of Southern decadence are Strindbergian themes moved to a lower latitude.

Indeed, anyone interested in realistic drama "written in tears and blood" inevitably becomes fascinated by the plays and life of Strindberg. Strindberg, in his dramas and autobiographical works, shows us not only the tears and blood of the creative process, but the sinews where they were produced. It was through Strindberg's plays and his collaboration with Nietzsche that an interest in psychology became the focal point of modern drama, long before Freud's influence had filtered through to cultural levels.

Strindberg suffered from and fought against a schizophrenic illness for a large part of his creative life. His

genius owes much to the heightened sensitivity characteristic of this illness, whether bitterly realistic in his early
career, or mystical and visionary in his later years. Strindberg transferred his illness nakedly into his work. His
productions are perhaps the best preserved record in
world literature of a creative genius' portrayal and search
for understanding of the psychotic process.

Understanding of human feelings may often be more
important than the comprehension of thoughts and symptoms. In the very year of Strindberg's final illness, Freud
started the search for the meaning of psychotic symptoms,
with an analysis of the memoirs of a German judge,
Daniel Paul Schreber. Schreber had written a journal
during his many years of schizophrenic suffering. This
journal, edited by the Schreber family to remove vital
but embarrassing information, became the source of a
theory which has exerted tremendous influence on psychiatric thinking. Besides their incompleteness, the
Schreber memoirs had many other deficiencies that rendered them of limited value to those seeking understanding of the feelings as well as the symptoms of the
schizophrenic.

First and foremost, there was the personality of
Schreber himself. He was a competent and compulsive
lawyer, very intelligent to be sure, but not blessed with
an abundant supply of imagination. In fact he tells his
future commentators and dissectors this when he says
poignantly that there are some sufferings which cannot
be described in words. It is the poet who has always attempted to express the humanly inexpressible in words,
with language expressive of feeling. While schizophrenia
is primarily a disorder of thinking, the accompanying disturbance of feeling is the area most amenable to help.
For a deeper understanding of the feelings of the mentally

ill, we must turn to those possessed of poetic imagination before and during an acute illness. Strindberg was a poet of the theatre, with a perpetual need to play out his illness on a stage larger than his own life. Although in many ways his psychosis was intensely personal, in other respects it was universal.

Strindberg was a man of enormous energy and insatiable emotional and intellectual curiosity. His interest in the external world was equaled only by a fascination with his own psychic functioning. With a desperate need and a unique ability to involve other human beings in addition to himself in his mental difficulties, he succeeded in maintaining a tenuous emotional contact with people which saved him from complete disintegration.

Relationships with women led Strindberg to disaster, yet provided his eventual salvation. The decisive event in his life was his first marriage with an unsuitable woman, whom he snatched away from a complaisant husband, reactivating old conflicts and fostering new complications. Gradually developing the feeling that his wife and other women were conspiring against him and persecuting him, Strindberg began a relentless search to discover why and how he had become what he was. With his penetrating intuition, he needed no Freud to tell him the importance of his childhood experiences, saying, "The early years are as important as the nine months that precede them."

Beginning a series of autobiographical works, Strindberg pursued his personality development and the origins of his illness back to his childhood years. Naturally, such early events seen through the haze of growing suspiciousness are subject to a large amount of retrospective falsification. Strindberg, however, displayed a ruthless sincerity in his self-dissection. The details of his work, while sometimes exaggerated with the distorted feelings of later years, have been found to be in remarkable agreement with his letters and the reminiscences of his contemporaries.

Almost all of Strindberg's collected work is autobiographical by his own admission. Seven of his prose volumes are composed of personal narrative meant for publication, but not for artistic gratification. In creating his greatest plays, he skillfully used fragments of his illness with shattering dramatic effect. We will analyze the major writings, extracting descriptions of feeling at various stages of Strindberg's illness, relating these feelings to biographical details as we discover the pattern of his suffering. Finally, we will use the results of Strindberg's self-analysis as guides toward fathoming the essence of the distorted and often mysterious feelings of the schizophrenic.

Strindberg's first major autobiographical work traces his history from his birth in 1849 until he received the traditional "white cap" of educational qualification at eighteen. It has been variously translated as "The Son of a Servant" or "The Bondswoman's Son," and was written in 1885-86, when difficulties with his first wife were approaching a climax. The second study, written in the same year, was titled "Fermentation" or "The Growth of a Soul," covering his career at the University of Uppsala between ages eighteen and twenty-three. Sandwiched in between this and the next significant autobiographical work is a book much beloved by the Swedes, called "The Red Room" (1879). It was written while Strindberg's family life was fairly serene, and it assured his reputation as a naturalistic novelist. While partly introspective, it is Rabelaisian in tone, being more concerned with social criticism than with self-analysis. The book describes Strindberg's period as a young Stockholm journalist, when he associated with the society of intellectual and artistic bohemians, whom he satirizes with a pen dipped in irony rather than reproach. Written largely to shock the burgeoisie, it provides little information about his emotional maturation.

In the autumn of 1887 Strindberg traced the development of his persecutory feelings in a remarkable book that he later regretted writing and which he published with great reluctance. It was written in French, a language in which he was unusually proficient for someone of Nordic background. The French title, "Le Plaidoyer d'un Fou," has been translated as "The Confession of a Fool," but is more exactly rendered as "A Madman's Defense." His devastating, acute illness was still seven years away, but troublesome delusions were already forming. Written in the form of a novel, the book represents the apologia of a paranoiac not only sincerely seeking an explanation for his own turmoil, but also feeling guilty over the suffering he has caused others.

Schizophrenia is a disease of long duration, during which acute symptoms may appear only at intervals. In the years between 1887 and 1894 when he suffered his catastrophic acute schizophrenic reaction, Strindberg brilliantly incorporated his developing delusions in his most famous plays, "The Father," "Creditors," and "Miss Julie." Then his illness, which had been insidiously increasing in intensity, burst forth in incapacitating form, and from 1894 to 1897 his creative productions ceased, except for books related to studies in medieval alchemy. Fortunately for a posterity eager for further understanding of the psychotic process, Strindberg kept a daily journal describing his feelings and sufferings during these frightful years. When his persecutions abated and he re-established contact with reality, Strindberg wrote two books titled "Inferno" and "Legends," utilizing quotations from the journal which described the illness and his heroic and ceaseless struggle for recovery.

"Inferno," taking its title from Dante's hell, is probably the finest, most perceptive portrayal of the frightening panic felt by a schizophrenic that has ever been preserved. Gone is the form of a novel; gone also are the elaborations of past events. Strindberg stands exposed to his imaginary persecutors, alternately battling and cringing, a hunted man fighting desperately for relief. In "Legends" the disease is beginning to burn itself out; we are permitted an intimate glimpse of the process by which a recovering schizophrenic comes to terms with his symptoms, finding solace in a reality reconstructed according to his own needs.

Strindberg's illness eroded his personality, rather than sapping his productivity. Vestiges of the illness remained as character traits that did not greatly interfere with his work. As previously, he was able to utilize his disturbance as subject matter for his plays. "The Road to Damascus" dramatizes the religious revival that aided in his recovery. However, the social disintegration that accompanies every schizophrenic illness increased his shyness, making him more taciturn and withdrawn. Strindberg was now middle-aged. The convivial drinking days of his youth would have passed, even if mental illness had not intervened. Now hatreds were soothed, and passions were converted into the silent devotions of the aging. Strindberg still needed love, but he found substitute satisfaction in the proffered adulation of the public, which in his youth he had scorned.

His last autobiographical works were written after the dissolution of his third marriage. Strindberg was back in his native Sweden, alone with his remembrances and regrets, and more inclined toward good works than toward self-analysis. The book "Alone" (1903) is important in showing the residue of his illness in its quiescent phase. Solitude and difficulty in relating to people he accepts as a punishment for past misdeeds, part of the price of atonement if he is to be saved. Distant memories of the acute illness were still treasured at this period, and in the "Blue Books" (1907-1909) Strindberg compiled a series of Biblical epigrams inspired by his religious experiences, designed to aid mankind and his fellow sufferers.

Belatedly feted by his countrymen, Strindberg ceased his wanderings and spent his remaining years in Stockholm, secluded from his admirers but thoroughly enjoying the thunderous applause. Each evening he read from a Catholic prayer book and prayed in front of a Buddhist shrine. At the end, clasping a Bible to his breast, he died saying, "All that is personal is now obliterated. I have done with life and closed the account. This is the only truth."

Strindberg, more than any other sufferer from mental illness, stands as a monument to human capacity with its ceaseless drive to comprehend. We will follow the course of this tortured genius from the zenith of his fame to the nadir of his psychotic panic, using his self-descriptions as an aid to the deeper understanding of the feelings and symptoms of the schizophrenic insane.

Previous studies of creative artists have stressed the search for psychological origins of the creative process. We are not primarily concerned with this question, being content to utilize the perceptions of genius without dissecting its origins. Other writers have explored the problem of whether creative talent can continue to prosper during mental illness. These studies, although fascinating as intellectual exercises, lead to little new knowledge or greater understanding. This book is not a study of co-existence, but of intuitive perception. We are interested in what Strindberg contributed to an understanding of the feelings of the insane, and how he used his talents to transmit psychology to modern drama.

STRINDBERG

THE ORIGIN OF PSYCHOLOGY IN MODERN DRAMA

CHAPTER ONE

The CHILDHOOD *of the* ARTIST

It is part of the hero's myth for men of genius to portray themselves as misunderstood and long-suffering in childhood. This excusable failing is shared by Strindberg, but his particular brand of personal realism gives his self-revelations an amazing candor, allowing his childhood reminiscences to remain valuable psychological documents.

"The Son of a Servant," Strindberg's first autobiographical work, is the saga of a son who never felt that he could get enough from his mother. Strindberg blamed and loved his mother in the same breath, a situation now described as ambivalence. Ambivalence is sometimes defined as hatred for someone who is otherwise loved, and this description applies perfectly to Strindberg's relationship to his mother with one important exception—otherwise loved —and desperately needed. Modern descriptions of himself as a little Oedipus would have made him smile, for he early penetrated beyond that facile and deceptively complete explanation of human behavior. Strindberg's craving for maternal care was one of his weaknesses and yet one of his saving graces. It made him suffer and led him to commit sins, but it kept him likable in spite of his transgressions.

Only at rare intervals was Strindberg aware that the emotions of the past must be understood in tune with the

realities of the present. Growing difficulties with his first
wife were what motivated his search for past understanding, resulting in his series of autobiographical works. Yet
Strindberg failed to recognize this connection; instead, he
blindly accused his mother of instilling within him a false
ideal of womanhood, which resulted in the tragic choice
of Siri Von Essen as his first wife.

In retrospect, he felt that his mother had cheated him
almost from birth. Strindberg was a premature infant, a
fact often romanticized by his biographers. Perhaps he
was also an unwanted child—this only his parents could
confirm, and they never expressed themselves publicly.
From the beginning he had an acute awareness that atti-
tudes were more important than events in his personality
development. Becoming aware of himself as a separate
person was a painful experience, as it is for most people.
The first feelings he could recall were fear and hunger.
He had many childhood phobias which were related to
later fears. These included fear of darkness, falling, and
being beaten, phobias which did not prove incapacitating
in childhood or adult life, until they became associated
with his schizophrenic illness.

Twenty years before Freud, Strindberg analyzed the
importance of parent-child relationships for future personality development, particularly the mother-child interaction. He realized early that a child learns and assimilates
the external world largely through the process of identification with his parents. As a child grows, he finds that
his parents will no longer satisfy all of his needs. This is
a painful experience for him, and it challenges the child
to imitate his parents and try to do for himself what his
parents formerly did for him. Skills of parents and significant people in the environment are thus made part
of the developing child's personality by identification.

This is a cumulative process, since the child, when confronted with an unknown skill or person, will assimilate it by identifying it with something already known. The child has a craving to imitate his parents because they hold him in high esteem in spite of his imperfections.

Of imperfections Strindberg as a child had an abundant supply. His sister remembered him as querulous and defiant, suspicious of injustice, and at the same time shy and sensitive. Yet, of course, his parents loved and encouraged him and attempted to tolerate his quixotic temperament. Actually, they influenced his development far more than he cared to admit.

From his steamship-agent father, Strindberg incorporated into his personality aristocratic and fastidious tastes, without his father's plasticity for compromise. Although a rather stoical Swede who preferred peace and quiet, his father had some taste for the aesthetic, enjoying musicales, cultivating geraniums, and reading widely in the European classics. Biographers of Strindberg have emphasized that his father was constricted in his home environment by the circumstances of his marriage. Strindberg himself pitied his father for being bound down to family life, as if a man with twelve children could be an Icarus. His was a morganatic union with a wife of much lower social position, a relationship that was legalized only two years before Strindberg's birth.

Despite his wife's humble social origin, Strindberg's father was devoted to her and to his children. His wife was a former domestic servant and waitress, no disgrace in itself, but a past that her famous son never forgave her. The human bondage that such a union may lead to has been picturesquely described by Somerset Maugham, but Swedish servant girls are often of different disposition and inclination from their English counterparts. Strindberg's mother Ulrica was more puritanical than promiscuous, preferring that bovine type of existence in which children are a boon, and religion the supreme consolation; all of which can be restful, if at times dull. She had three illegitimate children before her marriage in 1847, and bore a grand total of twelve, five of whom died in early infancy. To Strindberg's siblings she seemed to be a generous, non-punitive individual, efficient enough for the family's survival, if not wise enough to assist in assuring Strindberg's future tranquility. She completely lacked a respect for learning or any poetical sensitivity; she was more interested in tangible good works than in enriching her soul.

Naturally, even an understanding imaginative mother without a home bulging with other children would have had her hands full with young August Strindberg. Imaginative sons may not have imaginative mothers, but they demand much from them just the same. And Strindberg, with an inordinate need for affection, never stopped demanding. He was adept at maneuvering favors for himself, but he never managed to get that little extra which children in large families delight in extracting.

Ulrica's attitude toward her son was conditioned by August himself. As Kurt Goldstein has so convincingly demonstrated, a mother's response depends upon the type of child to whom she is responding. Strindberg was a touchy, sensitive child, with a perpetual chip on his shoulder. The suspiciousness which was to blossom forth into full-blown paranoia was already nascent in childhood. As early as he could remember, he had a preoccupation with injustice. He was always afraid of being accused of something he did not do. Any person he could not confide in seemed like an enemy to him. All of these traits he attributed to a nervous temperament inherited from his mother, whom he described as excitable and occasionally violent. In addition, he was very egotistical, always speaking of his resentment at having duties instead of rights.

Strindberg started his self-analysis during childhood. As with all future self-vivisectionists, as a child "he began to take a pleasure in self torture." Even in early adolescence it was written about him that "He suffers from the desire to do himself an injury, and finds almost a pleasure in self torments." Self-abnegation became a ritual, and martyrdom was seized upon as a means of gaining attention from his peers. His prose and dramatic works abound in examples of early reveling in masochistic delight. Unfortunately, he sought martyrdom as a penance for real and imagined transgressions, without first fully enjoying the sensual pleasure of his sins.

What Strindberg resented most in his childhood was the family's lack of emotional understanding of his rapidly developing perception. He felt that as a future poet he should have been nurtured like a tender plant, rather than treated like an ordinary youth. The resentment took the form of a railing against the material poverty he had suffered. At times he realizes that the family situation was not as bad as he pictured it, and his sister has informed us how August overemphasized the material poverty of the home. Despite occasional bankruptcies and constant changes in monetary circumstances, servants were always present in the house. Strindberg sometimes went to bed without food, not because of a shortage, but due to his fastidiousness. Summers were spent in the countryside, providing some of the most treasured memories of his childhood. He would ape the nobility at the Royal Castle, and dream the Prince and Pauper fantasies later used so skillfully in "Miss Julie."

The harsh, impersonal schooling of the mid-nineteenth century, with its forced feeding of Latin and its respect for beating, was not a milieu in which young Strindberg could flourish. With characteristic brilliance, he traced many of his adult character traits to the effects of the molding he had received in school. As an adult, Strindberg expressed opinions on every subject without restraint. He tells us that in childhood he would not speak in class even when he knew the answers, out of anger at the insensitive school system. He believed that his later garrulousness was a reaction to this former reticence. The hostility created by the school atmosphere could have one of two outlets—it could be externalized into a pursuit of sadistic pleasure, or transformed into a hardened conscience. Strindberg was a dependent boy (he compared himself to mistletoe, a climbing plant that must always seek support) who could only rid himself of anger in sudden cataclysmic outbursts after long intervals of internal seething..

As a schoolboy, Strindberg was so enamored of the study of the Gestalt of the outer world that he rarely paid attention to its constituent parts. When his surroundings seemed uncongenial, he dwelt in the realm of his ever-widening fantasy life. Giving free rein to his imagination, Strindberg did not yet recognize that the artist must remain partly constricted by current reality to allow him to develop his fantasy life, to delve into universal fantasies and mold them according to his gifts. However, these completely free excursions of the imagination sharpened his intuitive powers, leading him to an important discovery of Freudian psychology—the importance of feeling, and how feelings are connected with and influence ideas. "It is undoubtedly difficult to find out the real facts about anything—behind each thought there lurks a passion."

During these formative years, he felt that his mother was morbid and hysterical; she was possessed of spiritual pride, and her idealized wisdom was only a facade. Yet, when he felt lonely, or experienced the anger of others, he would use prayer to conjure up her soothing and enchanting image. Strindberg describes his mother as being a preserver, a source of warmth, and the eternal ideal of protectiveness. Every son has magical expectations and wishes centered on his mother. Maternal love has a selflessness and a purity that is eagerly sought after in other women. With most men there is a rude awakening to the bitter truth that no women are as altruistic and protective as Mother seemed during their infancy. When this happens, latent hostility often reaches conscious expression. Strindberg blamed his mother for engendering Madonna worship within him. It is certainly true that his relationships with women, beginning at age twelve, had a Madonna-like quality that was to plague him for the remainder of his life.

Strindberg's mother died of tuberculosis when he was thirteen, causing a reaction of sickening guilt instead of normal mourning. He was due to inherit one of her gold rings. The materialistic craving that he felt for this gold trinket at his mother's deathbed was to torture him in the sleepless nights of later years, and is reminiscent of similar guilt felt by other spiritual sufferers such as Gandhi. Strindberg's mother was a very religious member of the Pietistic sect, and she died exhorting him to live a godly life.

Only the naive interpreter would explain Strindberg's relationship to his mother solely on the basis of the Oedipal legend. Their connection went much deeper than that, being more a relationship of dependency and longing. He remembers shrieking like a drowning man when informed that his mother was dead. Insensitive

though she was to his developing poetic talents, her passing left an emptiness Strindberg was never able to fill.

One of his departed mother's legacies was a quest for
omniscience. No longer content with observing the Gestalt in nature, he searched for the wonders within. Strindberg learned all the varieties of plants in the Stockholm
flora, and started the chemical experiments which were
to become so important in the symptoms of his later mental
illness. Ironically, though his scientific endeavors were
designed as a monument to his mother, it was her passing
and his freedom from her oppressing religiosity that enabled him to be less timid and more searching after scientific knowledge. Later, Strindberg considered his psychosis as a punishment for having penetrated the secrets
of nature, and after his recovery he railed against science.
His mother had taught him to believe in faith as a
substitute for logical reasoning. Abandoning this in adolescence, he came to believe in it fervently during his
schizophrenic illness, when any renewal of scientific investigation coincided with a recrudescence of his terrifying symptoms.

The character of Strindberg's childhood experiments
is interesting in relation to his subsequent feeling of
being persecuted by an electrical influencing machine.
Investigation of the properties of electricity became his
passion. When he was twelve years old he built copper
and zinc batteries, later progressing to construct an electrical machine out of a spinning wheel. The house was
soon filled with Leyden jars, and plans were made to
construct a perpetual motion machine, which naturally
proved to be unsuccessful.

As Strindberg struggled to discover the nature of the
physical world, his father remarried before his year of
mourning ended, creating much criticism in the family.

This new crisis coincided with puberty when dormant sexual feelings were awakened. Becoming estranged from his stepmother, August experienced retaliation in the form of material deprivation. Religion came to his rescue, fulfilling the needs of this turbulent period in the absence of his mother's protectiveness. First, God was needed to combat the sexual feelings incapable of gratification. A book on the horrible consequences of masturbation terrified him and warned him that the only cure was Christ. Secondly, newly-acquired Christian feeling enabled him to endure privations and turn the other cheek. Finally, his stepmother was also a Pietist, and an interest in religion became a means of getting close to her.

Religion also helped him stave off feelings of adolescent depression. Strindberg prayed in the beautiful solitude of Haga Park, hoping that Jesus would seek him and free him from sin and burdens. He railed against the pursuit of Mammon which satisfied only sinful desires and passions. Recognizing his own penchant for egotism, he felt that only the austere introspection of the anchorite would save him. Yet, Strindberg longed for the stimulating companionship of intelligent contemporaries, and felt himself wasting time in caring for his younger siblings.

Religion served all of his purposes except reconciling him with his stepmother. Rejected by her, he obtained solace in a Madonna-like relationship with the landlord's daughter, sensing that it was her support rather than her love that was essential to him. Gradually the morbid clouds of his religiosity started to lift. Reading the sermons of Theodore Parker, Strindberg discovered that happiness was possible without believing in Christ and constantly fearing hell. He continued praying, but only out of habit. As his self-esteem rose, pietism and asceticism departed. Perhaps it would be nice to have fun and accumulate sins, and worry about suffering for them later. Strindberg now discovered an additional source of release in the conscience-soothing effects of alcohol.

When he was seventeen, a summer position as a tutor in the islands outside of Stockholm brought him into contact with cultured people, broadening his intellectual and social horizons. Shakespeare intoxicated him with his brilliance, and Strindberg early appreciated the bard's psychological acumen, feeling that the tragedy of Hamlet resembled the sorrows of his own life. Finally, at eighteen, in May of 1867, he received his "white cap" of educational qualification. To the ordinary youth this event represents a time of commencement and prospicience. To the introspective Strindberg, it was an occasion to look backward, and review the formation of his personality. Feeling that "a man's character is his destiny," his characterological analysis is largely concerned with doubts, fears, and weaknesses. Each liability seems to be counterbalanced by an asset. Despairing at this futile attempt to view himself objectively, Strindberg speaks almost in the terms of modern ego psychology. All people really acted parts. "And where was to be found the central 'ego,' the core of his character? The 'ego' was a complex of impulses and desires, some of which were to be restricted, and others unfettered." Already Strindberg was a determinist, feeling that he was destined to repeat his childhood behavior patterns. "So he stepped out into life—in order to develop himself, and still ever to remain as he was."

The real and imagined oppressions of childhood were over. The magical recollections of the summer at Drottingham Castle had begun to fade. In the distance were future expectations of artistic creativity. Strindberg's childhood had determined many things about his future career. First, his writing would always be intensely personal, and at its best bound to his native Sweden, that had spawned him and given him such a fitful beginning. Secondly, the core of his future mental illness was already present, together with the defenses and the means of recovery. There were his innate suspiciousness, his heightened sense of injustice. There were his copious fears, indicating a generous reservoir of free floating anxiety. There were his desire to probe the secrets of nature, and his passion for electrical machines that later returned to persecute him. There were his delight in self-punishment, his search for martydom. There was his intuitive genius in introspection, providing a painful blessing.

Finally, there were the parents, who shaped his growth. From his father Strindberg obtained his aristocratic and compulsive habits, his love of learning, of domesticity, and of the aesthetic. From his mother came his religious pietism, a search for the spiritual, and a delight in penance and superstition. Nothing affected his life more than his mother's leaving it; although her tenure had been brief, her influence was timeless. Carrying into adult life an idealized image of his mother as what a woman should be, Strindberg found only ersatz replacements in his wives. Then, rebelling against his almost desperate dependency on women, he came to champion the cause of mysogyny.

More than anything else, as he became an adult, Strindberg possessed a sensitivity unique in the creative artist. Nuances of feeling that passed others by touched him deeply. It was a gift that enabled him to obtain an emotional understanding of his complex childhood that was fantastic in its depth. It allowed him to free his imagination, to take his place in the twilight zone between fantasy and reality where the creative artist functions, and it permitted him to describe his feelings during a devastating schizophrenic illness, soothing his tortures and aiding in his recovery.

CHAPTER TWO

The IMPATIENT YEARS

Most people prefer to forget their adolescent years, looking backward with shame and regret on this early period
of searching uncertainty. The artist, however, realizes like
Goethe that every experience in life is part of a continuous quest. Strindberg, concerned with the reasons why
the passing years had failed to bring him emotional balance, subtitled his autobiography of these groping years
"Quo Vadis?"

He found few answers at Uppsala, where he was a typical university student. All through this phase Strindberg possessed a youthful intensity, with its customary
lack of proportion. Instead of quietly absorbing Western
culture, he experienced violent and undisciplined passions, seeking consolation in others' expressions of unrest. Older and steadier citizens, especially those in authority, were Philistines. Strindberg was yet too young
to appreciate the quiescent Goethe, who, in a balance
between the classic and romantic, had found the touch-
stone to understanding the essence of life. Like young
Schiller, before Goethe had governed his passions, Strindberg felt that life must have causes and purposes. Schiller
expressed these sentiments through the portrayal of
Karl Moor in the play "The Robbers," a character young
Strindberg identified with so strongly that he sought to

play the part on the stage, and thus transmit his personal unrest to others.

Strindberg studied at Uppsala, a center of traditional learning of more inspirational value to a training theologian than to a future dramatist There he developed a great reverence for Swedish traditions and a fervent longing to work within their boundaries. But he abhorred the Uppsala provincialism, which prohibited youth from effecting changes in tradition. He wanted to challenge and change everything, although he still lacked the means and the originality to do so.

At that time, calling on professors in a frock coat and seeking guidance was one of the accepted procedures of learning, especially for students in difficult financial straits. With typical stubbornness, Strindberg refused to make up for his pecuniary difficulties by becoming a sycophant. He was often lethargic, and prone to episodes during which he bemoaned the evils of civilization like a perpetual adolescent. Yet he read omnivorously and achieved a high degree of erudition despite these difficulties and his financial inability to attend lectures. Of special interest is his first contact with the works of his countryman Swedenborg, later to become his redeemer, but whom he now considered quite mad.

At the University there developed patterns in his interpersonal relationships which were to continue throughout his life. He was capable of forming quick and close individual friendships, but eventually succeeded in alienating most of his friends by argumentation and erratic behavior. Strindberg desperately needed and sought the approval of friends. He used them to test the value of his work and the reality of his artistic perceptions. Sometimes, pathologically suspicious of their motives, he discarded them with the ruthlessness of a politician. Reconciliations were rare; instead he would abjectly seek the approval and advice of other friends, easily finding more takers because his fellow students were fascinated by his intellectual versatility. At Uppsala, Strindberg was a member of the first of a long series of literary groups he was to frequent in later life. The group was called the "Runa Club," where worldliness was regarded as the supreme evil and primitiveness as the ideal. Strindberg and his fellow students shared a reverence for primitive life without the slightest understanding of its complexities. Many of these societies still exist. They serve the purpose of a sounding board for the exchange of literary ideas with a sympathetic audience. Psychologically they act as a kind of literary Alcoholics Anonymous, providing support for each of their members by attempting to build a mature confidence out of the conquer-the-world grandiosity characteristic of youth. Strindberg, flushed with prospects of success, recognized the assistance of the club in combatting his own consummate egotism.

Unfortunately, just as Strindberg began to derive some pleasure from life at Uppsala, lack of money forced him to return to Stockholm and live once more on the bounty of his family. Required to seek employment, the position he obtained was, ironically, as a teacher at his alma mater, possessed of bitter memories of his own restrictive and insensitive education. Observing the formless minds of his young pupils, Strindberg already felt what Nietzsche later confirmed for him, that society propagated a type of slave morality where children "were taught to ask nothing about life and then told lies about heaven."

Strindberg's career was still formless. While he pined to be ready to create, and he knew where the raw materials or, as he said, "ultimate resources" were, he did not as yet know how to get at or use them. "There lay and fermented in my mind a quantity of experiences, perceptions, criticisms and thoughts without any order," Strindberg tells us. Worthy of notice is that "experiences" and "perceptions" head the list. Increasing self-absorption frightened him. He thought of the heritage of madness shared by painters and poets of the past. Even at this early stage, he was terrified of his perceptions, which could lead him to great creative art or topple him over the precipice into madness. It is difficult to empathize with the complex feelings of a young creative artist on the brink of greatness, and foreseeing madness. The fight to follow the instincts, and yet adjust to society. To revel in changeableness, and yet to be resented for it. To be hated by the stolid disciples of necessity, yet envied by those with old bodies and young hearts. Strindberg sought a profession rooted in the pursuit of pleasure and imagination, without the usual subservience to reality.

It was the old battle between realism and romanticism which all creative men pass through, and all fear. Those who take the scientific direction use their imagination for relaxation. Even in the scientist flights of fantasy remain as a reminder of the essential dualism inherent in man, no matter how steadily he pursues the unitary ideal. Ernest Jones describes the battle fought by Freud, who achieved an unstable compromise. Freud struggled to subdue the romantic in his nature, losing the fight late in life, when his books read more like creative art than science. Strindberg's resolution of a similar conflict determined the foundations of modern drama. As a young student he recognized that romantic literary works were ineffective because they were emotional without being passionate. Freeing of the passions for dramatic effect required a subtle blending of the romantic and the realistic. The ideal solution Strindberg summarized thus: "The emotions should have full play, but must be under the control of good taste."

Fortunately, Strindberg had access to sympathetic advice during this struggle. He lived in the home of a cultured Jewish physician, Dr. Lamm, as a medical apprentice. When Strindberg informed the doctor that "The romantic was in his blood, but the realistic side of him was about to wake up," he was addressing a kindred spirit who had once been in the throes of a similar conflict. They had long fatherly discussions as Lamm tried to solidify the interest Strindberg had shown in medicine. The Lamms were a family who maintained an interest in books and the theatre, and in which the children had freedom of expression. Here Strindberg learned the secret of the survival of the Jews, and empathized with their creative homelessness. "To be without a native country, which is regarded as such a hardship, has this advantage, that it keeps the intelligence alive and vigorous." Here there came to him the painful realization that to be an intellectual vagabond, it was also necessary to be economically independent.

Although Strindberg enjoyed chemistry and some of his other studies, medicine represented more a continuation of the search to understand nature's secrets than a desire to be of use to his fellow man. As Strindberg engaged in animated conversation with the actors who visited the home, Dr. Lamm knew that the craving for the aesthetic was winning. Finally, Strindberg left his medical apprenticeship observing that "his imagination was set in motion and his memory refused to work," and that "the reality of cauterizations and flowing blood was ugly." Seeing the real tears and blood of people under stress had undoubtedly quickened his powers as a psychologist. It is more than accidental that Strindberg, Ibsen, and Chekov, masters of the psychological drama, all studied medicine. Strindberg's plays especially show the influence of medical training; they are written with the skill of an experienced clinician and they dissect human emotions at crucial periods of life. Strindberg's preoccupation with the effects of birth and death on his characters may represent a vestige of his medical experiences. While he never formally returned to medicine, he remained fascinated by drug effects and the development of medical psychology. He later read the works of Charcot and Bernheim, experimented with morphine, and dabbled in hypnosis.

Strindberg chose the theatre as a means of self-expression, as the medium through which he would vent his fears and unrest. The shyness was still present, and it was later to become magnified into agoraphobia, a fear not only of people, but of open places. Apparently he used his appearances on the stage to conquer these fears, for he speaks of his acting experience as "doing violence to his shyness." The future father of realistic drama decided on a dramatic career because "The theatre was an unreal world which enticed one out of the tedious real one." Strindberg's first phase was, like Schiller's, a polemicizing one. Translating Schiller's treatise on the theatre's idealistic purposes, he agreed that the theatre must be an educational and reforming, almost a revolutionary, force.

Later, frustrated by the mechanical and stilted acting style then in vogue, Strindberg rebelled unsuccessfully, and resolved to become a playwright after his failure as an actor. It was a terrible blow to him to be denied access to the stage which he needed to act out his emotional conflicts. He felt depressed, because he was unable to express anger at the theatre manager for not acclaiming his thespian talents. So, he swallowed his hostility in the form of opium and alcohol in a suicidal gesture. Awakening refreshed, he composed his first dramatic work in a feverish ecstasy similar to Coleridge's state when he wrote "Kubla Khan." Strindberg's description of his dramatic inspiration is in close accord with the descriptions of other creative artists, as Ernst Kris has summarized in the fine study "Psychoanalytic Explorations in Art." Inspiration seems to come suddenly from beyond with one great burst, like a thunderclap during a storm, and the lethe-like state which follows is never forgotten. "When the work was finished he drew a sigh of relief, as though years of pain were over, as though a tumor had been cut out."

Like many other geniuses, Strindberg compared the creative process with childbirth. "He felt a kind of peace like that which follows parturition. Something or some-one seemed to be there, which, or who was not there be-fore; there had been suffering and crying, and now there was silence and peace."

Strindberg's first dramatic work was a minor effort soon consigned to oblivion. Terrible struggles with women and mystical religious experiences were needed before his writing would mature. Even the first efforts were dominated by religious confusion and sexual turmoil. In the beginning of his career he contemplated a series of religious plays, which he returned to later when he re-covered from his psychotic illness. With characteristically mixed feelings, he thanked God for having granted him poetic gifts, then conceived of a tragedy to be called "Jesus of Nazareth," which would "shatter the divine image and eradicate Christianity." Having a strong con-science and being by nature a Puritan, Strindberg sought unsuccessfully to free himself from the burden of as-cetic morality. Lacking a sense of humor (a quality which has made his plays particularly attractive to the Ger-mans), he found few outlets for his sense of sin.

There is usually a type of confident anxiety present in the launching of first literary productions. Strindberg felt this prior to the presentation of his first play, "In Rome," at the Theatre Royal, Stockholm. Before leaving Dr. Lamm, he journeyed to Copenhagen with Lamm's son to see the Thorwaldson sculptures. The career of this talented artist, who had lived in self-imposed exile in Rome and once destroyed his own masterpiece, fascinated the groping, self-destructive Strindberg. Thorwaldson's smashing of his own statute provided the climax of Strindberg's play. Walking along the bank of Lake Malar on opening night, he felt as though he were standing under an electric machine. It was the first time he compared feelings of anxiety to being permeated by electric currents. Anxiety then became more intense and progressed to fear. Shocked that he had revealed his feelings so openly, Strindberg seemed to fight against the compulsion that was to make his plays a life-long confession. In response to criticism, he made intemperate retaliations, and was soon ostracized by his fellow artists. The dangers of self-revelation that he had feared were now real. Frequently, one of the early signs of approaching insanity is a fear of losing control. Ashamed and baffled by his attacks on friends and supporters, Strindberg began to fear he was losing control and he doubted his sanity for the first time. Writing to the director of a mental hospital for advice, he was reassured that all sensitive people have emotional crises.

It was time to withdraw and meditate like the Buddhists that he later came to respect so much. Back with his family, he found an unexpectedly sympathetic haven that restored his equilibrium. Later Strindberg expressed the feeling that his triumphs had been achieved unaided. But there is little doubt that he had a deep appreciation of the contributions of family and friends, when he said, "Every personality is not developed simply out of itself, but derives something from each with whom it comes into contact, just as the bee, gathering honey from a million

flowers, appropriates it and gives it out as her own."
His contact with his older and more daring brother,
Axel, a stipend together with admiration from the dying
King, and belated interest and encouragement from his
father raised Strindberg's confidence and self-esteem. Feeling that he had not yet experienced enough, he again
sought to free his passions for artistic usefulness without
succumbing to their horrendous implications. Study of
others who had done this successfully, such as Dante,
Shakespeare, and Goethe expanded his creative horizon.
Ibsen's "Brand," the current sensation, upset him. With
further agitation he read Kierkegaard's "Either-Or," at
once appreciating Kierkegaard's powers as an intuitive
psychologist which have only recently been extolled. We
can imagine how Strindberg was a sympathetic audience
for Kierkegaard's portrayal of suffering as a form of enjoyment, particularly the tortures of unrequited love. Kierkegaard also taught him that "Life was a perpetual inter-
change between pleasure and pain."

When this period of meditation was completed, Strindberg tried other avenues of self-expression to free his
artistic creativeness. Associating with a group of painters,
he expressed his brooding in painting gloomy seascapes.
He invoked that muse unsuccessfully, and wrote some
poor poetry. But the theatre remained his best hope, and
he persisted despite disappointments, like having his plays
rejected and having the stipend stopped after the King's
death. Gradually, Strindberg began to realize that artistic,
like social, evolution is a slow process. He learned that
great art must be molded out of uncertainty in the crucible of frustration. While ordinary men searched for
security and certainty, he came to understand the artist's
credo that the joy of life lay in the pursuit, not in the
fulfillment.

Strindberg was now on the threshold of the unfortunate

marriage which, catalyzing his gradually developing paranoia, culminated in an acute schizophrenic illness many
years later. Already we can discern why he eventually recovered. Harry Stack Sullivan, the physician who had
more understanding of the feelings of schizophrenics than
anyone else, constantly emphasized the push toward mental health that these unfortunate people display. In Strindberg the recovery process was simplified because, feeling
himself to be on the brink of madness from late adolescence, he began this push long before becoming acutely
ill.

Intelligent, sensitive people often envy those of lesser
endowment who seem to live apart from complexity and
suffering. However, emotional conflicts are universally
present, and it is a weak defense to deny their existence.
Never content to adopt this defense, Strindberg always
strove to understand. His fantastic energy, intellect, and
perception were resources lacking in other schizophrenics,
enabling him to comprehend and gain strength from his
early sufferings, thus accumulating a cushion against disintegration. While he was acutely ill, Strindberg's world
seemed more painful, and even his thoughts were disturbed. Faced with this prospect, the ordinary schizophrenic develops a sense of inner and outer deadness, in
which he begins to feel that the world has come to an end.
Withdrawing from externals, the schizophrenic becomes
disinterested in his surroundings. His own place in the
external world is all-important—he has little contact with
outer realities except as they pertain to the distorted image he has of himself.

There are many reasons why Strindberg never reached
this end-of-the-world feeling so characteristic of schizophrenics. Despite his self-preoccupation, he had a de-
vouring interest in his surroundings. There was a fascina-

tion with botany, chemistry, medicine, and the depth perception of others. Strindberg not only had to know how and why he functioned, but also how and why everything around him functioned. Before the acute illness, he examined its precursors in his childhood. He was able to partially understand that feelings of persecution arose from within himself rather than emanating from the outer world. Thoroughly rooted in reality, when the world seemed distorted, he clung to the belief that he might be imagining things, and continued fighting against the easier course of believing that his persecutions were raising him above other mortals. While Strindberg later did share some of the schizophrenic's false feeling of grandiosity in the possession of superior knowledge, he retained a compulsion not only to inform others about his stereotyped delusions, but to portray his distraught feelings and sufferings.

Many schizophrenics reach an affectless stage, where emotions are no longer evident and other people are shunned. It is as if the struggles have overwhelmed them, and peace has been gained as a pyrrhic victory at the expense of the feelings. Strindberg's feelings remained passionate, and he never reached this stage. Always struggling to renew emotional contact with people, he never withdrew completely into himself. His turbulent and uncertain relationships with others during his formative years smoldered on throughout his life. Mixed feelings toward his mother passed into excessive love and hatred toward his wives; adolescent religious struggles became reverence for God, followed by disbelief. His feelings swung like an erratic pendulum, never functioning smoothly, yet never coming to rest. Thus were both Strindberg's personality and his creative gifts saved from extinction.

CHAPTER THREE

MATERNAL NEED
and
MARITAL SUFFERING

There is an old saying, "When a wise man goes to find a wife, he should take along a fool for an expert." Strindberg, unfortunately, was his own fool. Indeed, he titled the autobiographical description of these marital years "Le Plaidoyer d'un Fou," translated as "The Confession of a Fool" (or better, as "A Madman's Defense"). Written in 1887-88, when Strindberg was racked with thoughts of murdering his wife and then committing suicide, the book delineates an astoundingly accurate picture of the development of paranoia. Strindberg felt that it was a terrible book. Composing it because he expected to die shortly after its completion, he commented, "I had to wash my corpse before it was laid in its coffin." Kept sealed by a relative for five years, the book was not published until Strindberg had been violently attacked in the Swedish press.

"The Confession of a Fool" covers fourteen years of Strindberg's life, from the moments prior to his fateful meeting with Siri Von Essen (1875) to the time of his separation from her (1889). Written in the form of a novel, it moves from the raptures of love to the anguish and suffering caused by the battle against unjust suspicion. We see a curious blending of hatred projected onto others, and the beginning of terrible guilt and self-hatred. Although there is no evidence yet of schizophrenic thought disorder, there are obvious forebodings of approaching insanity.

But we are running ahead of our story. Before meeting his wife, Strindberg drifted through Stockholm for three years, occupying himself as a minor journalist. Later he wrote about this period in "The Red Room," hailed as a cynical masterpiece and one of the first realistic novels. Here revolt against society obsesses him. Using exaggeration and grotesques, Strindberg pictures the subterranean life of Stockholm, artistic, financial, and political. In unmasking others he did not, of course, conceal himself. The dominant Strindbergian themes of women and religion are already in evidence. The hero, Arvid Falk, also recently returned from Uppsala, is an oversensitive writer who must always stand outside society and is prone to a nervous disability cured only by a peaceful holiday in the Stockholm islands. Falk suffers from a hopeless Madonna-worship of women and delights in analyzing the Ten Commandments, pleading that the fifth has incriminated him. Yet, despite its autobiographical tone, "The Red Room" is further evidence of the incisiveness of Strindberg's perceptions about others. This is in keeping with the acting-out characteristics he possessed. This type of individual must involve the significant people of his environment in his own emotional turmoil. With deadly accuracy he penetrates the psychodynamics of others—this is necessary if he is to use them without their knowing it. Strindberg often boasted that he could talk to a person for a half hour and know all his emotions and thoughts. In "The Red Room" he used this for commercial success; later he used this uncommon ability for his own survival.

Finally he tired of drifting, a type of life longed for by the dreamy adolescent, but very uncomfortable when it is finally achieved. With the coming of discomfort, the revolt against society and the family ceases—the homey virtues once desperately avoided are now vigorously sought after. Strindberg needed a woman. His search was driven by common inartistic motives—dependency and biology. Domesticity might be artistically dull as it was for his father, but it did satisfy sexual and other needs in a quiet, peaceful fashion. Also, other girls were available to him besides servant girls.

Many years later Strindberg said, "What is woman? The enemy of friendship; the punishment that cannot be escaped, the necessary evil, the natural temptation, the longed-for misery, the fountain of tears which is never dry, the worst masterpiece of creation in white and dazzling array." Strindberg arrived at this disillusioned description of women after his marital experiences. In retrospect he felt that the meeting with his future wife, Siri, had been predestined. They were introduced by another girl, with whom he pretended to be in love. Looking for a maternal image from the beginning, Strindberg describes Siri as "a deliciously girlish mother," though maternal qualities later proved to be the least of Siri's assets. "This womanly tenderness, the secret of which none but a motherly woman knows, was a new experience for me," he tells us.

Psychoanalysts have not yet gotten firm hold of Strindberg, but those with Freudian orientation who have written about him have had a field day traveling down the Oedipal trail. Even the initial battles of Strindberg's stormy marital life were fought on Oedipal territory. Siri was married to an army officer, and lived with her husband in the same house where Strindberg had spent his childhood. As Strindberg rang the bell on his first visit, he described the hidden fear that his father might answer the door.

He adored Siri with the same Madonna-worship of his childhood. She was now the mistress of the house once guided by his mother, and at first this unusual circumstance precluded any sexual desire for her. He was afraid to pollute her with his passion. Strindberg says, "The instinct of worship latent in my breast awoke, and with it the desire to proclaim my adoration. The void that had once been filled by religion ached no more. The yearning to adore had reappeared under a new form. God was deposed, but his place was taken by a woman; a woman who was both virgin and mother."

That Siri was no virgin was proved by the presence of her three-year-old daughter. This, however, did not deter Strindberg, and he soon found further proof that she was a virgin-mother in disguise by learning from her husband that she was frigid. Indeed, in a childish way, Strindberg was unable to view the relationship between Siri and her husband as a sexual one. The psychoanalyst Frosch has shown how the average child cannot visualize his parents as sexual beings. The child views the goings on between his parents as follows—"other people do things like that, but my parents, never." Strindberg behaved in this way, trying very hard to excite Siri's compassion, wanting to be treated like "an ailing child." Homosexual undertones also pervade the description of his first meeting with Siri. Insisting that his ideal was the virginal woman, Strindberg further says that he could not have worshipped Siri as much if she had not been married. Later, as his illness worsened, he accused Siri of having homosexual relations with her friends.

Leaving his transient journalistic appointments, Strindberg now obtained a secure position at the Royal Library in Stockholm. Here there were bureaucratic orders that made him unhappy, but his scholarly predilections were encouraged. The intellectual probing of Strindberg's scholarship was fantastic in its scope and perseverence. He would always enjoy periods of intense mental concentration, followed by a communion with Swedish nature in the Stockholm islands. While at the Library, Strindberg maintained his interest in history, literature, and science, even studying Chinese for a year and writing a treatise on the relations between Sweden and China. In this historical study, widely acclaimed abroad, he wrote about himself even while discussing non-emotionally-charged material. The same preoccupations which possessed him throughout life are strongly evident here. First, there is excessive chauvinism, a glorification of the mother country that succeeds despite all adversity. Then there is a detailed discussion of religion. Religious feeling, Sweden, mother—these themes which dominated his later work already appear in an obscure historical study. Showing meticulous research in its compilation, this early work already contains value judgments, caustic comments, and typical Strindbergisms.

With his financial position now more stable, Strindberg's passion for Siri Von Essen developed rapidly. Many factors fostered the relationship in addition to biological attraction. To some extent Siri responded to his overtures for maternal affection. In another respect they were kindred spirits. Siri had a passion for the stage, and Strindberg was beginning his career as a playwright. They were both restless, Siri constricted in a dull marriage, and Strindberg because of his nature. Events and the complicity of others fostered their love and the development of Strindberg's illness. Strindberg's rival played the role of complaisant husband, making him feel guilty in winning Siri. At first he conceived of a conflict with the soldier husband in true romantic fashion—"the sword versus the pen." Then, sensing his own cowardice, he felt loath to engage in conflict and planned flight.

Guilt at stealing another man's wife proved to be a decisive point in Strindberg's illness. It later reached fever pitch, and persisted into the recovery period, finding expression in the play "The Road to Damascus." At the time, however, he did not feel he had sinned, since the woman was willing. "In love man is never a thief, he only takes what is given to him," Strindberg tells us, continuing, "The only time she gives unselfishly is when she betrays her husband. The faithless wife only gives to her lover that which she has stolen from her husband." Again we see an undercurrent of homosexuality—a preoccupation with the other man in the triangle. What is taken from him is just as important as the needs the woman gratifies.

Siri fulfilled another characteristic of Strindberg's pathological search for a wife. She needed saving. Like most perceptive individuals, Strindberg could sense unhappiness with great ease. Siri was described as "a soul in torment, a power wasted, a voice unable to make itself heard, just like myself." Strindberg lavished his attention on her. He interested her in literature, helped her to write, and encouraged her ambition to become an actress. Any woman is responsive to prolonged attention, especially if she is virtually ignored by her husband. And the more Strindberg encouraged her, the stronger their attachment became.

Finally she responded with erotic interest, and Strindberg fled in terror at this temptation. Even the cuckold was treating him as if he were a younger brother. On a boat speeding toward Paris, he started to panic, and for the second time extreme anxiety made him feel as if an electric shock had passed through him. Strindberg related panic to the "rising of suppressed memories." A woman on the boat gives him motherly attention and soothes him to sleep. "She radiated warmth, that warmth which a baby seeks in the arms of its mother—I seemed to have become an infant again." Despite its being so obvious, Strindberg's crying out for maternal attention possesses a dignity lacking in the maudlin outbursts of someone like Proust.

There is little doubt that during this episode Strindberg went backward to childish levels of functioning, as is typical in a schizophrenic breakdown. What is peculiar is his awareness of this regression, together with a craving for human companionship and a determination not to withdraw. In a desperate yearning for his friends, he tells the captain, "Have me put ashore or I shall go mad." Strindberg now discusses the subject of madness for the second time, at the age of twenty-six. Although the renowned Karl Jaspers, the most authoritative of the commentators on Strindberg's mental state, dates the first appearance of schizophrenia to the early 1880's when Strindberg was in his thirties, there is evidence in "The Confession of a Fool" that Strindberg passed through a brief schizophrenic episode in 1876. After a discussion of the phobias of his adolescence and a description of fugue or amnesia-like states, Strindberg reaches the conclusion that at times he had been subject to mental delusions.

Feeling that he has "the cunning of a madman," Strindberg seeks to bring Siri to nurse him by swimming in the cold October water and deliberately exposing himself to the wind in order to contract pneumonia. As he runs naked through the woods, hallucinations are approached. "The muttering of the junipers is almost like the whisper-

ing voices of women, telling each other secrets." Returning to a hostel, Strindberg sends a telegram to the complaisant husband, informing him that he is ill. "And from
that moment on I was prepared to die or go out of my
mind," he tells us. A priest converses with him, and,
filled with the picture of a contented salvation, he swal-
lows a bottle of pills, resolved to die. After good dreams
and a refreshing sleep, Strindberg awakens, believing in
the poet's version of *cogito ergo sum*—"I dream, therefore I exist."

The gesture is effective. Siri hurries to his bedside, and
treats him like a child. He comments—"and how sweetly
she played the part of a mother, the tone of her voice was
like a caress." Siri's arrival did not prevent a sudden erup-
tion of blatant evidence of schizophrenic disorder. The
landlady of the hostel believes that Siri is Strindberg's
sister because of their close physical resemblance. Strindberg observes, "Had my constant intercourse with Siri
affected the expression of her features?" This idea that
he could influence others solidified into a firm belief
eighteen years later, during his acute psychotic illness,
and even persisted into the recovery phase. Features of
that illness were already present. Though not actually
persecuted, he felt that he was being tested by some unknown force. Later he felt that he was in hell; now he
speaks of his sojourn in the woods as hours of purgatory.

It seems strange that someone of Strindberg's perceptive powers would not recognize the extreme disturbance
of his relationship with Siri, and the forebodings it con-
tained. But, as Freud pointed out, love itself, with its
unrealistic overestimation of the loved one, has some
of the characteristics of insanity. Strindberg recognizes the
common ground of love and insanity, when he says, "Love
and delusion are inseparable, and it is difficult to know

ourselves as we really are." In love, ratiocination ceases. It
is *après nous le déluge*, but unfortunately for Strindberg,
the deluge came before.

Yet, to give Strindberg due credit, he did try to extri-
cate himself, not because he had a premonition of future
discord, but because he saw the affair ending in a crime.
He told Siri, "That I love the woman of my choice is
my own affair, as long as my passion does not infringe on
the rights of another." He entreated her to keep their
relationship platonic. It was a losing fight. Visiting Siri's
husband when he fell ill, Strindberg in their bedroom
began to visualize the discordant couple as sexual beings
and felt justified in breaking up the marriage. Siri's
mother, seeing the situation developing toward its inevitable conclusion, begged Strindberg to be a kind guard-
ian to Siri and her child.

Later, when Strindberg felt that Siri was persecuting
him in an attempt to drive him mad, he tried to deny his
own part in the affair, accusing Siri of being a temptress
who had forced him to become her lover in spite of himself. As is usual during mutual recriminations, there was
justice on both sides. There is little doubt that Siri was
a rather predatory ambitious woman who recognized
Strindberg's talent and wanted him to write plays for
her. There is also no doubt that she encouraged Strindberg in his attentions. But, unable to see how unsuitable
she would be as his wife, Strindberg pursued her as the
answer to all his needs.

To understand so much, and to make such a horrible
mistake! It is one of man's psychic misfortunes to be im-
pelled to action more by need than by reason. Strindberg
longed for family ties; Siri sought to escape from them.
They were two people with Pygmalion-like fantasies. Siri
looked on Strindberg as a talented playwright whom she

would inspire to further her career. Strindberg, with his dependency needs, wanted to make Siri into a German hausfrau, who would be bovine and unquestioning, except when he chose to stimulate her, intellectually and otherwise. From the beginning he recognized that, as with his own mother, there was hatred beneath his love. He warned Siri, "Beware of the sick Lion. Don't come near his den or he will kill you with his caresses."

Come she did, in spite of the stigma of divorce, trading an unhappy marriage for one destined for disaster. After Siri had separated from her husband, Strindberg felt less attracted toward her. Already suspiciousness was developing. She was leading both her husband and himself to disgrace. He began to feel that "matrimony is a mistake and love is a sinful passion," but he resolved to marry her because he felt personal responsibility for Siri's dilemma. When Siri left for Copenhagen to establish residence for divorce, the theme of religion and mother was repeated again—she kissed him like a mother, and "her last embraces led him back to God."

The second part of "The Confession of a Fool" covers the period between Siri's separation from the baron and the time that her protuberant abdomen forced Strindberg to marry her, an interval of many months. It was a time of ripening suspiciousness, when the future delusions were visible in nascent form. An individual rarely develops paranoid ideas suddenly. They develop slowly, until all the intricacies of the fully formed plot are evident. To an outside observer it may appear that the development was sudden, because most paranoiacs in the early stage are silent. It is only when they start telling people about their suspicions that the world finds out.

Now disdaining the life of a mistress and housewife,

Siri immediately used her new freedom to pursue an acting career. While she had been married to an army officer of high birth, it had been impossible for her to go
on the stage. Actresses were still supposed to be wanton
women in that era, and respectable girls of the upper
class were forbidden to have traffic with the stage. Siri
adapted herself so skillfully and so quickly to the stage that
Strindberg became suspicious. Perhaps she really was a
"born wanton," and her success was not due solely to
her talent. Observing Siri indulge in the inevitable flirtation necessary to theatrical existence, Strindberg saw
some confirmation of his growing suspicions. He forbade
her to be photographed in suggestive poses, telling her
that success had made her coarse.

All this before they were married! Actually Siri's reputation as a good actress rankled Strindberg for two reasons. First, he was jealous, saying, "Her personality was
grafted on mine and was dominating it." Then, as he
did not find his own needs satisfied, his writing naturally
suffered. No man can allow a woman's success to take
the place of his vanishing talent. When in the midst of her
burgeoning fame Siri encountered misfortune, Strindberg
did not appear greatly sympathetic. Her daughter died
of encephalitis, and the paternal grandparents spread the
word that it was God's judgment. Immediately after, Siri's
mother died suddenly of heart disease, and again her
demise was attributed to divine retribution. Rather than
supporting her faithfully during this sad period, Strindberg felt that he had been the cause of these misfortunes,
and was worried more about his own salvation than about
her discomfort.

These stresses accelerated the development of his illness. When the child died, Siri understandably sought
some consolation from her former husband, whereupon

Strindberg suspected them of again sleeping together. Unable to produce any literary work, he accused Siri of sucking his blood, and stealing his thoughts for her own use. Although not quite like those of the full-blown schizophrenic who believes that others can read his mind, the delusions were beginning. When she asked for money shortly after sexual activity, he called her a prostitute, believing even now that she was the leader of a female plot slowly forming against him. The greatest of all the sins Strindberg observed in his future bride was a debasement of the maternal instinct. Yet he persisted: "I was powerless to lift her up, powerless to struggle out of the morass into which we had fallen. I resigned myself to remain tied to her, even if I had to witness and share in her downward course."

Then, from the maelstrom of despair and suspicion Strindberg was raised, as he would always be raised, by the smile of a child or by the approaching motherhood of his mate. Siri was pregnant, and she suddenly seemed pure again. Confinement turned her from a wanton into a saint, worthy of his adoration. As "Fortune was smiling at us with a tear in the eye," they were married. Before or after marriage it would always be all or nothing for Strindberg. Siri had to be either a saint or a sinner. The intermediate zone where most women belong was beyond his comprehension. Now, with a pregnant wife, all was serene. "What inexpressible happiness it is to be married," Strindberg says. "It is as if one had regained the home of one's childhood, with its sheltering love, a safe port after the storm, a nest which awaits the little ones."

Strindberg had taken his wife from another man who had defiled her, and he resolved not to corrupt her himself. Their marriage would be maintained as a pure relationship between two artists. His ideal was a complete union with freedom for both partners. They would sleep in separate rooms, meeting for sex by mutual agreement. Swedish couples still prefer single beds to double ones despite the cold winters, but Strindberg's scheme was not motivated by tradition. It was symbolic of his unrealistic aims, and part of his innate selfishness. Siri must ask no questions, yet must know all the answers. She must awaken his passions, yet be satisfied with solitude. Strindberg hated emancipated women, yet wanted to give his wife freedom from everything, including himself. As at Uppsala, Strindberg failed to understand the complexity present in simplicity, and he had to learn through bitter experience that there are types of freedom people hate as well as treasure.

Strindberg now became painfully aware that the maternal instinct was not only invented to help men recreate themselves in their own images, but was also a fundamental need that must be satisfied. Siri gave birth to a premature daughter who died two days later. It was the second child she had lost within a year, a terrible tragedy for any woman. Siri looked for some helpless creature to mother, and acquired a dog. Strindberg gradually worked himself into a fury over his wife's attentions to the dog. He protested so vehemently about the animal that the reason for his annoyance soon became obvious—Siri squandered maternal care on the dog, incensing Strindberg who wanted all the attention for himself. During this episode his behavior was so erratic that Siri started to believe he was insane.

Three years passed, of which Strindberg said, "At times I fancied I was living in a lunatic asylum, but one does not stand on trifles when one is in love." Whenever he was reasonable, Siri forgot all of his hostility and became maternal. When his suspicion blazed and association with him was impossible, Siri sought the companionship of other women. Then Strindberg was convinced that a conspiracy of females was forming against him. "They were trying to make me believe that all our unhappiness was due to my unstable nerves, and persuade me to consult a doctor," he said. As he became more and more hypersensitive in female company, he accused his wife of having homosexual relations with her best friend, a forty-year-old spinster, identifying her as the one who was turning Siri against him. Siri told Strindberg that he had a perverted mind, and the couple's sexual relations steadily declined.

Married life is destined for tragedy when both partners need the same things and search for them in each other. Underlying the passionate marriages of youth there are basic needs that determine the choice of a mate. Often when a passive man marries an aggressive, domineering woman, people comment on what a termagant the wife is, but some of them realize that he needs such a woman despite the price she exacts for her support. All men have dependency needs, nurtured in the long mother-son relationship that is unique to the human species. Women respond to these needs, within the limits of their own personalities and requirements. It was one of Strindberg's tragedies that he required more mothering than others, but he was sexually attracted to precisely the opposite type of woman from the one who could satisfy his needs. He pursued actresses who responded to his intellectual stimulation and were fascinated by his diversity and versatility, without understanding how much his talents were dependent on a steady supply of support. His first wife, Siri, was not the ideal "giving" type of woman he fantasied her to be. In fact, she craved affection herself. While the assuaging effect of another pregnancy saved the family situa-

tion from erupting into violence, Strindberg could not fill
the role of a father after the child was born. Instead, he
competed with the new infant for Siri's limited attentions,
begging for maternal care himself. When this was denied,
Strindberg complained that Siri was unable to realize his
ideal of motherhood. Actually, no woman could, since
his real mother had tried unsuccessfully to satisfy his
needs.

As Strindberg's marital difficulties increased in intensity, he began writing down observations on his own and
other marriages, with a view to using them as literary
material. Like Goethe, he could make love with one hand
and take notes with the other. Strindberg's motivation was
not psychological but financial—his family was growing, and
for want of other inspiration, he could write about marriage. It was an established institution, and the potential
market was a big one. Also, the subject had been opened
for clinical inspection by Ibsen, whom Strindberg stig-
matized as "the famous Norwegian bluestocking." Nora
of "A Doll's House" was the rage, and with his own
hatred and disappointment, Strindberg easily became the
apostle of a one-man anti-feminist movement. His own
torments neatly meshed with a topical subject. He may
have been slightly crazy, but he was no fool when it came
to fascinating subject matter. Strindberg would tell of his
own ideals and enmities, and demonstrate a remarkable
knowledge of love and marriage, despite his personal
disturbance. It is ironic that some of the best writers on
this subject, notably Balzac and Stendhal, had the least
satisfactory sexual adjustments. It is not that they knew
too much; they lacked the capacity to synthesize and use
what they did know.

Tormented by growing feelings of sexual inadequacy,
Strindberg's mind became a mélange of homo- and hetero-

sexual suspicions. His first defense was the proven remedy of making Siri pregnant again. A pregnant wife is too immobilized to indulge in infidelities. How often the magical sperm is used to re-establish masculinity when men feel threatened! When Siri suffers a miscarriage, Strindberg interprets this as proof of her betrayal, and begins looking around for the culprits, first male, then female. A male doctor had given her Swedish massage for back trouble, and, he suspects, other kinds of massage as well. He sees her kissing other women, and suspicion now grows into certainty. "Holy matrimony was degraded to legal prostitution." He can no longer picture his wife as an angel. Siri is now a perverted homosexual who is trying to drive him insane.

People who develop ideas of persecution often have concomitant homosexual preoccupations. This observation led Freud to suggest that paranoid symptoms develop as a defense against unconscious homosexual wishes. The author has shown that the association is a firm one, although this fact does not substantiate the claim that homosexuality is causally related to paranoia. Paranoid and homosexual feelings may be present in a wide variety of mental illnesses unrelated to schizophrenia. Strindberg's suspicions regarding his wife are not conclusive evidence of schizophrenia. Indeed, his mental breakdown was still several years away.

Why would Siri want to drive him insane? Perhaps, Strindberg thought, she wanted him put away so she could collect his money. Maybe she wanted to marry again. In any event, she was succeeding. A story appears in the newspapers stating that he is insane. The years of turmoil have had their effect on both partners. Strindberg contemplates suicide with cyanide; Siri, although a success on the stage, has begun to drink heavily. Slowly,

Strindberg begins to doubt the legitimacy of his own children. Furiously agitated, he consults a doctor who advises a trip abroad in order to escape complete insanity. At last, Strindberg thought, Siri would be removed from the proximity of her lovers, and they would have a chance to recapture some of the lost tranquility of their courtship.

When mentally ill people travel for respite, they never really succeed in leaving their conflicts behind. Strindberg was now firmly convinced that his wife wanted to get rid of him by putting him away in a lunatic asylum. With such a fixation, one can imagine what the trip was like. Their peregrinations lasted six years, taking them all over the Continent, and wherever they went, Strindberg had the feeling that his wife was informing friends in Sweden of the progress of his insanity. With brilliant insight, he described his feeling of being kept like a lunatic, saying, "I was on the verge of insanity and the first symptoms of persecution mania showed themselves." Only when Siri treated him like a child or was pregnant, was there any peace. When he complained to his Parisian friends of her persecutions, their reassurances had no effect. The reality of her persecutions had been firmly established in his mind.

Once again, this time in Switzerland, the paranoid delusions already focused on Siri reached out their tentacles to include others. Siri was poisoning the minds of the hotel inhabitants, turning them against Strindberg. "Our new abode was a kind of purgatory where I was continually watched by twenty-five women, who incidentally furnished me with copy for my book" The book was titled "Married," one of his best sellers, and one which created additional conflict. It was a collection of short stories about marital life. Rather than a bitter denunciation of the institution, the book contains a surprisingly benign description of Strindberg's fantasies of the ideal marriage, as well as acting as a catharsis for some of his pent up rage. Strindberg proclaims: 1) Woman's place is in the home—Man protects, woman fulfills. 2) Man must be dominant, since he is endowed with greater intelligence and ability to understand the deeper things in life. 3) Equality of the sexes is folly; women who try to compete with men end in disaster. All this is very moral, and strangely reminiscent of another eminent Victorian's formulation of female psychology—Sigmund Freud's. How, then, did the book get him into trouble?

Legend has it that the Queen of Sweden read the book and was the instigator of the legal action for blasphemy which was filed against Strindberg and his publishers. It must be remembered that this was not modern Sweden, where only the elderly go to church and there is a reputation for sexual license. This was late nineteenth-century Sweden, a rather puritanical country where Cotton Mather might have felt at home. Popular indignation against Strindberg rose; the book was confiscated by the public prosecutor and the author and publisher were ordered to appear in court. The first story, "The Reward of Virtue," was chosen as the main issue. Strindberg was indicted for committing blasphemy by mocking God's word and the sacraments. What he actually was guilty of was calling Jesus a rabble-rouser and attacking transubstantiation, things that others had been doing with impunity for hundreds of years.

Trembling in Switzerland, the wildly suspicious Strindberg received news of the furor his seemingly harmless little book had created in Sweden. What frightened and amazed him still more was his growing reputation in Sweden as a corruptor of youth. In reality it was not an age when the young bought books to be corrupted by.

The publicity was bad for his literary reputation and for business, as well as being murderous to his psyche. Of course, there was a right of redress. At first Strindberg was afraid, and decided to stay in Switzerland and let his publisher face the suit alone. A fervent plea delivered in person by the scion of the Bonnier family finally made him courageous, and he decided to return to Stockholm for the trial. The fact that Siri refused to come was used as more evidence to prove that she was against him.

On the basis of what we already know about Strindberg's personality, we can predict what would have been the best type of reception for him. As a boy he looked for martyrdom, seeming to derive pleasure out of painful situations. Ostracism was the punishment he expected and most desired. After crying frequently on the trip from Geneva to Stockholm, he was feted as the hero of the populace. There was a homecoming celebration at the Central Station, followed by a special performance of his fantasy play, "Lucky Peter's Journey." The acquittal after a four-week trial was greeted by another public ovation. Strindberg's response to the mayhem was pregnant with meaning—"My shot went off, but it was too much for the gun. The pitcher has sprung."

The crowd always had to have its sensational hero, but Strindberg was under no illusion that the people who cheered him were the ones who bought his books. The self-appointed guardians of public morals would inevitably prove to be more powerful. We must also remember that Strindberg was a puritan by inclination and in his personal tastes. His ideal was the quiet, pastoral existence next to God, united with a nobly planned and not too inquisitive woman. To be accused of blasphemy cut especially deep; his reverent mother would never have forgiven him. The person who suffers punishment has often been looking for it; Strindberg's successful avoidance of punishment only heightened his sense of injustice. Psychology sometimes moves in strange directions. If he had been convicted, he probably would have felt relieved. Ample evidence for this supposition is provided by Strindberg's feelings during his acute psychotic illness. He felt guilty of corrupting the morals of the young with his writings, and that this was one of the reasons why "the powers" were punishing him. In "Legends," Strindberg enters a museum where he sees a medal struck off in honor of his acquittal twenty years before, and the sight fills him with remorse. The persecutions of his schizophrenic illness were viewed as part of the punishment that should have been meted out by the court when he was tried for blasphemy.

Strindberg's biographers have been quick to blame his later illness on the traumatic events of this trip. His subsequent mental deterioration has been traced to the strain of the trial. It is an old and natural human failing to seek one cause for one event. It makes life simpler. Even when Strindberg was insane, he was too wise to accept such explanations. He realized that single events usually have multiple causes. There is little doubt, however, that the trial did act as a miniature *coup de grâce,* solidifying his paranoid delusions and increasing his venomous hatreds.

The paranoid delusion almost always has some basis in reality. Why? Because the person with ideas of persecution eventually manipulates his environment to the point where people are forced to persecute him out of self-defense. For instance, Strindberg, having grievances against his wife and other women, used his suspicions as material, writing a book about married life and railing against emancipated womanhood. The book was published and resulted in legal prosecution. Strindberg was

now able to say that people were really against him because he was a mysogynist. The fact that he was prosecuted
for blasphemy and not for his opposition to female emancipation was not important to him. During an illness of
this type, subtle distinctions seem insignificant. Strindberg
now felt certain that his delusions had a basis in reality.

Further misinterpretation of reality followed Strindberg's return to Switzerland, as his illness worsened with
great rapidity. Occurrences in the external world began
to assume deeply personal significance for him. For example, Ibsen had written a popular play called "The
Wild Duck." Strindberg reads it and becomes convinced
that the central character is a portrayal of himself. The
chief character in the play doubts the paternity of his
children. Such doubts had been growing in Strindberg's
mind for a long time. Now Ibsen convinces him that Siri's
former husband was the father of his first baby, and that
this scandal has been used for dramatic effect. He contemplates suing Ibsen for slander. Strindberg was often on the
verge of getting himself into trouble over his delusions,
but always managed to avoid incarceration by restraining
himself at the last minute.

The remaining years of the marriage were filled with
tremendous suffering for both parties. As Strindberg's
suspicions turned into hatred, he accused Siri of associating with more and more disreputable company. Convinced of her present infidelities, he projects them back
into the past. He eavesdrops in the hope of catching her
in illicit sexual affairs, and tries to find out the names of
his rivals. In Switzerland he opens her mail and in Sweden
he deputizes his brother to check on her past love affairs.
His hatred assumes homicidal proportions, almost resulting in violence. Calling Siri a prostitute, Strindberg
attempts to drown her in a river, but is held back by the
thought of the children's grief. Accusing her of torturing

him and inventing the myth of his insanity to hide her transgressions, Strindberg beats her, desisting when his heart softens again at the appearance of their children.

The battle with Siri gradually becomes a vendetta, with Strindberg striving only to clear his name. When he accused Siri of slowly poisoning him with cyanide, even his friends believed that he was insane. Yet he still needed her desperately. During a trial separation he wrote her passionate and loving love letters, feeling "like an embryo prematurely detached from the umbilical cord." In the epilogue to "The Confession of a Fool," Strindberg dedicates himself to a crusade to discover the origins of his sufferings, making use of psychological methods. "A crime has been committed in secret or else I was mad. I must know the truth," he says, appealing to the reader to give a verdict whether or not he is a lunatic.

In the final stage of incurable paranoia the victim blames everything on others, assuming no personal responsibility for his deeds. Strindberg vented his hatred easily, but turned it inside himself with equal facility. All through "The Confession of a Fool" there are poignant descriptions of the suffering Strindberg felt at causing pain to others. Strindberg always sought to understand the consequences of his illness as well as its causes—how they affected others as well as why they affected him. Toward the end of "The Confession of a Fool" he has begun to feel guilty of some secret crime he cannot identify. Ironically, this growing guilt provided Strindberg with his sole source of respite. From childhood, self-punishment seems to have given him a type of pleasure. One of the things to be learned from Strindberg's illness is that masochism, or finding satisfaction in suffering, may often be a blessing, acting as a safety valve to prevent further disintegration.

During these years of marital discord Strindberg wrote

some of his best and most perceptive works. After the
separation he felt isolated and sought out others like
Nietzsche, who had been wronged by women and might
be sympathetic. With varying degrees of subtlety, he continued to pursue his diatribes against women, using his
work as a catharsis for his suspicions. Needing a maternal
woman, Strindberg had not chosen wisely but he believed
that he had learned his lesson well. Adapting "The Confession of a Fool" for the stage as "The Father," he un-
masked woman for what he felt she was, a predatory creature whose sole aim was man's destruction. Strindberg's
finest play thus arose phoenix-like from the depths of his
illness and the ashes of his first marriage.

CHAPTER FOUR

DOUBLE MADNESS:
STRINDBERG *and* NIETZSCHE

Dearest Doctor.—I will, I will be mad. Not without perturbation did I receive your letter, and I thank you for it. More rightly wilt thou live Licinius, if thou wilt always steer forth on the high seas, nor cowering fearfully before the storm, cling too closely to the coast.

In the meantime all hail to madness!

Adieu, and keep in kind remembrance
Your Strindberg,
(the best, the highest God)

Strindberg wrote this in the fall of 1888 in reply to Nietzsche who had sent him a very peculiar letter. Nietzsche replied:

Herr Strindberg,
Eheu! No more! Divorçons
The Crucified One.

A few days later friends came to take Nietzsche away from Turin and place him in a mental hospital in Switzerland. When Strindberg heard of this tragedy, he was frightened lest these letters be used as evidence of his own insanity. Fortunately, they were not published until released by Nietzsche's sister in 1913, after the philosopher and the playwright were both deceased.

It is remarkable how brilliant insane people have an affinity for each other. This does not appear to be true of those of lesser intelligence who lack creative talent. In mental hospitals, schizophrenics of average endowment will exchange ideas and feelings only when compelled or influenced by outsiders. With brilliant people there is a hunger for communication that transcends the illness. Strindberg formed two such liaisons, one with Nietzsche, who influenced his illness and work, and the other with the teachings and mystical spirit of Swedenborg, who acted as the "redeemer" in his recovery from acute psychosis.

Strindberg realized that Nietzsche was mentally unbalanced, although he did not recognize that even at the start of their correspondence Nietzsche was already demented. Strindberg wrote of Nietzsche, "I believe he makes me blind, for my brain from overexertion is like a wound, but he certainly makes me crazy, for the unheard of egotism in his books has conveyed itself to me—We will undoubtedly meet in Gheel" (a large open colony mental hospital in Belgium). Later, after Nietzsche had been hospitalized, Strindberg expressed the opinion that the greatest mind of the century had been incarcerated, protesting, "He is as sane as I am." Strindberg was accurate on all counts except in his prediction of a meeting. First, the consummate egotism of Nietzsche's writings did influence Strindberg's illness and his work. Then, although at this time Strindberg was not as psychotic as Nietzsche, he was deteriorating rapidly and was to become acutely ill within a few years.

Strindberg and Nietzsche were introduced in correspondence by the Danish critic George Brandes, who had been the first to popularize Nietzschean ideas in his Copenhagen lectures. Brandes, an independent acquaintance of each man, recognized their similar viewpoints and predicted that they would become good friends. Nietzsche was the master of the prose invective, Strindberg the genius of dramatic vituperation. They had a mutual mysogyny, and Brandes felt they should be united to fight the Ibsen craze which he disliked. There was a similarity in Nietzsche's claiming of power in his poetic grandiosity and the power of mental telepathy already being claimed by Strindberg. Besides, Brandes felt Nietzsche's elated and confident mood might cheer up the conscience-stricken and frequently depressed Strindberg.

What Brandes could not know was that apart from other literary contributions, both Nietzsche and Strindberg were leaving valuable descriptions of the psychotic process in their writings. Nietzsche's insanity was caused by advanced syphilis, which had first made its appearance in 1881, according to Lange Eichbaum's monumental work on human genius. By 1888, when the Nietzsche-Strindberg correspondence took place, Nietzsche was close to his final rupture with reality in 1889, after which he remained insane and incoherent until his death in 1900. The author has summarized Nietzsche's poetic description of withdrawal and recovery in the psychotic process. Niezsche described his feelings of estrangement with a poignancy only Strindberg has equaled. As a depth psychologist Nietzsche earned the kind comments of Freud, who credited him as a precursor. Freud paid tribute to Nietzsche as a promulgator of the instinct theory and as an analyst of civilization's discontents.

Strindberg's introduction to Nietzsche's work in their garbled correspondence proved to be of vital importance to the development of the modern theatre, for it was through Strindberg that Nietzsche, the brilliant fore-runner of contemporary psychoanalytic theory, exerted his influence on modern dramatic literature. Dramatists like Eugene O'Neill were far more likely to come into contact with the theories of depth psychology through the Strindberg-Nietzsche coalition than through reading books on psychology.

Tracing the development of this half-productive, half-psychotic fusion is a fascinating experience. Strindberg and Nietzsche had many things in common personality-wise, in addition to their insanity. Both were raised in a religious atmosphere—Nietzsche's father had been a minister and Strindberg's mother a staunch Pietist. In adult life they revolted against tradition and condemned their previous asceticism. Yet both retained a puritanical streak which personality change could not eradicate. In 1888 Strindberg was in an atheistic phase, and the Antichrist preoccupations of Nietzsche found a receptive audience. Both men, although shattered by traumatic experiences with women, were able to utilize their misfortune in the writing of their best work. Nietzsche, still smarting from a rejection in his one and only love affair with Lou Salome, had written in *Zarathustra,* "Thou goest to women? Do not forget thy whip!" Strindberg, seething with paranoid suspicions regarding his wife, used these feelings as material for his best plays. Nietzsche thus provided Strindberg with fuel for his burning rage against women. We can imagine how eagerly Strindberg, thirsting for revenge against his wife, took up Nietzsche's whip in addition to his own weapons. Strindberg and Nietzsche, both failing to achieve sexual adjustment, used their claims of supreme power and strength as compensations for dependency neither could admit—Nietzsche on his sister, and Strindberg on his wife and mother. Strindberg and Nietzsche shared a penchant for considering themselves misunderstood martyrs. We have seen how this tend-

ency plagued Strindberg from childhood. Nietzsche likewise reveled in martyrdom. If people had rushed to
become his converts instead of his detractors, he would
have felt lost. As Nietzsche's illness progressed and his
grandiosity increased, he considered his life a martyrdom,
finally calling himself "The Crucified." During Strindberg's recovery from schizophrenia, he too approached an
identification with the martyrdom of Christ.

And they found a companionship in their loneliness.
Sometimes people with the unique gift of alienating
others, find companionship together. Both Nietzsche and
Strindberg had a craving for the friendship and advice of
their peers. Later, they disdained criticism with a vehe-
mence that revealed its origins in need. Nietzsche has become the hero of generations of depressed adolescents
who have Nietzschean needs, but no understanding of his
philosophy. To some extent, this was one of the purposes
Nietzsche's theories served for Strindberg.

What were the essential things Strindberg derived from
Nietzsche? First and of crucial importance was the support of his own views and feelings. As a creative artist,
Strindberg possessed an innate capacity to be profoundly
original without outside assistance. But in order to produce, he needed sympathetic supporters to demonstrate
to him that he was not alone in his unorthodox opinions.
Such reassurance built his self-esteem and gave him
strength to write. When Strindberg felt persecuted, Nietzsche seemed like a witness for the defense against his
enemies. When Strindberg became preoccupied with the
class struggle in his plays and his autobiography, he
learned that Nietzsche also had contempt for the lower
classes and "slave morality." Being Germanic, both were
interested in the origins and potentialities of willpower.
Strindberg, having studied the hypnotic method of Bern-

heim and having read Charcot's books, was fascinated by
Nietzsche's psychological excursions. Most of all, Strindberg found in Nietzsche a fearless man who dared to
preach openly the rights of men over women and the
strong over the weak. In fact, Nietzsche's outspokenness
so impressed Strindberg that from the beginning his admiration for the German philosopher was unrestrained.

The beginning occurred in May 1888, when George
Brandes introduced him to Nietzsche's work. Soon Strindberg was ending all letters to his friends with the admonition, "Read Nietzsche." Brandes, afraid that he had caused
harm, urged Strindberg to tone down such unqualified
enthusiasm, commenting, "Much of his (Nietzsche's) doctrine seems to me far less original than it appears to you
and him." Strindberg was angry at the world and at the
religion of his mother, and Nietzsche preached and predicted the downfall of civilization and Christianity. What
could be better? He described Nietzsche as "the most independent and strongest mind who lives today." Sometimes Strindberg was objective enough to see some of
Nietzsche's psychotic grandiosity in himself, and it scared
him. But he still said, "I see in Nietzsche the most modern
and liberating mind of us all."

The correspondence was started by Nietzsche, who had
just completed an autobiographical fragment, "Ecce
Homo," which was written in a jargon that gives ample
testimony to his mental difficulties. In the advanced stage
of syphilitic grandiosity, Nietzsche considered "Ecce
Homo" so significant that it had to be published in four
languages at once. Through some acquaintance with
Strindberg's work, Nietzsche recognized in Strindberg a
perceptive psychologist capable of understanding his feelings. After reading "The Father" in French, he was certain that Strindberg could translate the descriptions of his

misery. Nietzsche wrote, "Between ourselves, in order to translate my 'Ecce Homo,' a poet of the first order is required. It is an expression, a *raffinement* of feeling, a thousand miles above the capabilities of the ordinary 'translator'—I am a psychologist." Then the insanity becomes evident. "It is something of supreme importance. For I am powerful enough to break the history of humanity into two parts." Nietzsche later asked Strindberg to translate his works into French, and sent him a copy of *Thus Spake Zarathustra.*

Strindberg never did translate Nietzsche's works; he apologized, saying that he had to earn money and could only accept translations at the standard rate. There must have been no hard feelings after Nietzsche read Strindberg's impression of *Zarathustra.* "Without doubt you have given mankind the deepest book that it possesses, and what is more you have had the courage, and perhaps the urge to spit these splendid sayings in the very face of the rabble. I thank you for that." After rereading a complimentary copy of "The Father," Nietzsche was ecstatic not only about the contents, which agreed with his own mysogynist concepts, but he also recognized it as the founding work of naturalist drama, just as Zola's writings had created the realistic novel. Nietzsche called "The Father" "that masterpiece of hard psychology," and wrote to Strindberg, "I read your tragedy twice over with deep emotion; it has astonished me beyond all measure, to come to know a work in which my own conception of love—with war as its means, and the deathly hate of the sexes as its fundamental law—is expressed in such a splendid fashion." With excellent judgment Nietzsche recommended that Strindberg present "The Father" to Zola, and also try to get it produced at the new avant garde "Theatre Libre" in Paris. Zola had some reservations to the effect that the play was too starkly realistic without a "social setting," but he recognized and encouraged Strindberg as his dramatic counterpart. The revolution in dramatic literature created by "The Father" was about to begin, with Nietzsche providing the *élan vital.*

The remainder of the Nietzsche-Strindberg correspondence was a succession of letters expressing mutual admiration, with a felicitous exchange of books and unqualified praise. In a few months Nietzsche was completely insane, so that Strindberg had no effect on his work. But the impression that Nietzsche produced on Strindberg was deep and long-lasting. The distinguished French playwright Arthur Adamov describes Strindberg as a direct descendant of Nietzsche. With romantic exaggeration, one Strindberg biographer states that Nietzsche destroyed Strindberg's first marriage. Actually, both were ill long before they corresponded, during the waning days of Strindberg's marriage and Nietzsche's rationality. The effect Nietzsche had on Strindberg's private life was to make him more daring in his paranoid attacks. Strindberg wrote to Brandes, "My spirit life has received in its uterus a tremendous outpouring of seed from Friedrich Nietzsche, so that I feel as full as a pregnant bitch. He was my husband."

While Strindberg was gestating dramatic masterpieces under Nietzsche's influence, his real children were suffering. He attacked his wife with increasing viciousness and started preaching blasphemy at home, calling Christianity a religion for "women, eunuchs, children and savages." The pious Siri struck back, castigating him for trying to corrupt his own children as he had already corrupted Swedish youth with his writings. This did not deter Strindberg, who said that he felt "like an overcharged Leyden jar." Even the news of Nietzsche's hospitalization failed to slow Strindberg's attacks, although he brooded about it for a long time. We must remember that he had been frequently preoccupied with thoughts of insanity since adolescence. Just prior to his own acute psychotic episode, he ruminated once again on Nietzsche's insanity as he had done five years previously. Strindberg's adoption of the idea of the Nietzschean Superman colored his psychosis. During his acute schizophrenic illness, when he felt controlled by "the powers," he believed that the purpose of "the powers" was to make him into a Nietzschean Superman. In the book describing the beginnings of his illness, Strindberg wrote, "I was educated by three Buddhists, Schopenhauer, Von Hartmann, and lastly Nietzsche." As he started to recover, Strindberg became a convert to Swedenborg's Catechism, comparing Swedenborg's "Higher Man" with Nietzsche's "Superman." Thus Nietzsche's influence persisted all through Strindberg's illness, ending only with the religious recovery. Afterwards, Strindberg became a penitent and felt that he merited eternal punishment for fostering Nietzschean ideas. He expressed penitence that his own criticism of Christianity and God had once been as intemperate as Nietzsche's. He even nurtured vague feelings of guilt that his play, "The Father," might have helped drive Nietzsche insane.

It was Nietzsche's destiny to influence Strindberg's work during his greatest productive period (1887-1890), in the writing of the plays for which he is most revered. While not responsible for the practice, Nietzsche was directly responsible for the theory of naturalist drama, a theory which sired contemporary dramatic literature. The first naturalist drama, "The Father," was written before the beginning of the Nietzsche correspondence, and was one

of the first works Strindberg sent to his newfound sup-
porter. Strindberg was tremendously frightened by its implications, writing, "I don't know if 'The Father' is an
invention or if my life has been so, but I feel that at a
given moment not far off, this will be revealed to me, and
then I shall crash either into insanity from agony of conscience, or into suicide." The fact that two such eminent
contemporaries as Nietzsche and Zola considered the play
not merely a fragment of insanity, but a dramatic masterpiece, provided Strindberg with essential support.

It is very doubtful that any of Strindberg's friends realized how ill he was, and how "The Father" used the content of his illness directly, without alteration. The play
was written in the first two months of 1887. At this time
in his personal life, Strindberg was checking on his wife's
fidelity, had doubts about the paternity of his children,
and felt that his wife was trying to drive him insane. In
Strindberg's play, the Captain is driven insane by his wife,
Laura, who makes him suspicious about the paternity of
his daughter.

The shattering brilliance, mastery of dramatic technique, and unexcelled horror of this play have never been
equaled. Zola was appalled at the play's directness. Despite its obvious exaggeration and frenzied distortion,
Strindberg's portrayal of female machinations has enough
truth to be ruthlessly effective. The play has a perfect
unity of time, place, and action. The principal characters
are sketched without wasting a word, and the battle begins
from the first lines. The wife is portrayed as a female Iago,
as evil incarnate, who, without boasting about her nefari-
ous plans, thoroughly enjoys her destructiveness. Skillfully, she persuades her husband's friends, his doctor, even
his beloved daughter, of his insanity, winning everyone to
her cause. Gone are the Shakespearean props like handker-

chiefs, overheard conversations, and anonymous letters. Suspicions can develop quickly. Madness is not caused by something mystical; its potentialities exist to a greater or lesser extent in everyone. Strindberg shows us one case, his own. The Captain is an intelligent scientist, unfortunately readily suggestible and possessed of a nervous temperament. He must always know the truth and can never doubt without unrest. If he knew that his wife was unfaithful, he would feel at peace. Doubt slowly drives him insane. Finally, Laura informs him that she has arranged to have him put away in an asylum. All his suspicions of her plotting are suddenly validated—he heaves a burning lamp at her, thereby assuring evidence for his commitment.

Strindberg not only realized that he was using "The Father" as a catharsis for the murderous impulses of his illness; he also knew the way out of the approaching tragedy. An old nurse is able to pacify the Captain, persuading him to accept a strait jacket. Soothed by maternal care, he reminisces about the happy times he had previously enjoyed with the wife who has destroyed his reason. A woman could be both a savior and a tormentor. Had his mother lived and been sympathetic, had he been able to find a woman to gratify his need to remain dependent, he might have been saved much suffering.

Strindberg's contemporaries saw "The Father" as a war of the sexes, written with cold-blooded fury for dramatic effect. In his first play Strindberg had been frightened that he had revealed too much of himself on the stage. What makes "The Father" a masterpiece is not entirely its personal revelations of hatred; it is also a study of pathos. Whereas "The Confession of a Fool" had been an apologia, "The Father" was, in addition, a plea for understanding. Unlike the more pedestrian Zola, Strindberg knew that sadness and tragedy need no social milieu—they are universal, existing in castles as well as in slums. In all locales woman could be a treacherous seducer, and at the same time the source of redeeming warmth. Certain laws of life it was useless to fight against. Man was always cheated in trying to create children in his own image. He sowed the seeds, but woman raised and controlled the children. Again Strindberg appreciated all aspects of the unique mother-child relationship. Mothers provided the sustenance and protectiveness necessary for growth, yet selfishly guarded their young as personal property.

The strong conquer the weak; only the psychologically fit survive. Strindberg's main failing seemed to be weakness, but in a savage world weakness may also be a crime. Like the Captain, Strindberg was resigned to accept his insanity as punishment for his known and unknown sins. Coleridge once observed that people like Laura were driven by a "motiveless malignancy"—Iago in "Othello" and Claggart in "Billy Budd" are other prize examples. Yet, in the midst of the pain these individuals cause, there is beauty; in the midst of anguish there is truth. With his poetic insight, Strindberg distilled both beauty and truth out of suffering.

Prefaces to great works often exert a tremendous influence on literary development. Wordsworth, in the preface to "Lyrical Ballads," inspired and defined lyric poetry. Shaw, in his monumental introduction to "Saint Joan," showed how important historical figures could be both universal and human. Strindberg's preface to his most widely performed work, "Miss Julie," transmitted Nietzschean psychology to modern drama.

Strindberg's reverence for Nietzschean ideas developed after "Miss Julie" was written. Hence, the theme and content of the play were not influenced by Nietzsche. However, the remarkable preface was composed after the play's completion. This polemic introducing the text became an exposition of the psychological theories introduced in the play. While it was the later Nietzschean grandiosity that provided Strindberg with support, fortunately it was the early brilliant Nietzschean perceptions that influenced his dramatic theory. They seemed to crystallize out the ideas of his plays, transforming Strindberg from a skilled practitioner of naturalistic drama into a prophet of the contemporary theatre.

With typical daring Strindberg firmly stated that he was creating a new drama, modernizing from and changing content. The content would be life, "which now seems so brutal, so cynical, so heartless.'" Strindberg says, "I find the joy of life in its violent and cruel struggles, and my pleasure lies in knowing something, and learning something." The only available way to understand life is through "unreliable instruments of thought which we call feelings." Perhaps some day, Strindberg tells us, thoughts will control feelings. Until then, people will be imperfect, but vital.

Strindberg has learned that life has no absolutes, no single cause and effect relationships, no pure passions. Therefore, verisimilitude in the theatre depends on conflicting motivation. He says, "An event in real life—and this discovery is quite recent—springs generally from a whole series of more or less deep lying motives, but of these the spectator chooses as a rule the one his reason can master most easily, or else the one reflecting most favorably on his power of reasoning." People like the valet Jean in "Miss Julie" are of indeterminate character, "oscillating between love of distinction and hatred of those who have already achieved it." Through the

character of Mephistopheles in "Faust," Goethe had
shown with rare wisdom that what may appear as consummate evil also contains elements of the good. From
his traumatic marital experience, Strindberg came to realize that even the women who persecuted him had noble
qualities.

Strindberg's characters might have similar hopes and
fears, but they were not homogeneous. He described them
as "a blend of old and new," vacillating as they attempt
to borrow strength from one another. Such a description
of character broke with classical tradition and appealed
especially to the French avant garde, one of the reasons
why Strindberg's plays first became popular in Paris.
French writers usually trace their lineage to a particular
historical style, treating their characters according to patterns established by Corneille, Racine, or others. Strindberg denigrates this custom as a middle-class notion
"synonymous with a gentleman fixed and finished once
and for all—who invariably appeared drunk, jolly, sad."
"This manner of regarding human beings as homogeneous
is preserved even by the great Molière," Strindberg tells
us. That people never ceased to grow by adaptation was a
discovery of the late nineteenth century. Coming as it did
before Darwin, classical drama had no conception of how
interaction with the environment could result in change.
Nietzsche and Strindberg had both been enthusiasts of the
Darwinian revolution. Nietzsche viewed the struggle for
existence in cosmic proportions; Strindberg had seen it on
a personal level. Nietzsche widened Strindberg's scope,
and in the resultant naturalistic drama, individual conflicts were related to universal struggles.

Since Nietzsche and Strindberg were both frustrated
lovers, it is not surprising that their collaboration con-
tained a preoccupation with female psychology. Psycho-

analysts now speak of the "castrating woman" who seeks to appropriate man's power for herself. In the preface to "Miss Julie" Strindberg discusses the woman who strives to compete with men, "selling herself nowadays for power, decorations, distinctions and diplomas." Like Freud, Strindberg felt that this type of woman violated natural law, and he picturesquely described her fate. "Frequently, however, they perish in the end, either from discord in real life, or from the irresistible revolt of their suppressed instincts or from foiled hopes of possessing the man." These tragic women have become all too frequent in our society. Perhaps this is an additional reason for the renaissance of interest in Strindberg and his probing into their archetypes.

Strindberg disagreed with Nietzsche and Zola in one important respect. The idea of guilt had no place in Nietzsche's system; the Superman was above eternal law and not liable to punishment. In Zola's novels guilt is expiated by relating sin to environmental cruelty. Strindberg remained obsessed with guilt, especially during the recovery from his psychotic illness. He wrote, "The naturalist has wiped out the idea of guilt, but he cannot wipe out the results of an action—punishment, prison, or fear." Later Strindberg said, "There are crimes which are not entered in the law-books, and they are the worst; for them we punish ourselves, and no judge is so severe as we." This sense of guilt gave Strindberg a humility even in the presence of supreme confidence. He finished the preface to "Miss Julie" with the statement, "I have made an attempt. If it proves a failure, there is plenty of time to try over again."

The attempt was a brilliant success. All the assets and liabilities of modern drama resulted from this amalgam of Strindberg and Nietzsche. Life was not inherently ugly, but grotesqueness was one of its features that could not be ignored. The disciples who misused the wise advice gleaned from "Miss Julie" emphasized the sordid, distorting the purpose of naturalistic drama. Even during his periods of illness Strindberg maintained a sense of balance in his plays. He was able to portray psychological conflict on the stage because he was writing from the perceptions of his own turmoil. His plays are startlingly real—they never smell of newsprint. True, Strindberg was influenced by literary trends (Zola) and by Nietzsche. But his tragic illness was his own, not something he read about and adapted for want of material. An intensely personal plea for understanding is always more effective than a second-hand message. This is equally true of the work of Strindberg's brilliant descendants. O'Neill composed his most effective plays ("Desire Under the Elms," etc.) before becoming acquainted with popular psychology; Williams wrote his best play, "The Glass Menagerie," long before he began his psychoanalysis. Critics have noted how O'Casey's later work became tainted by a forced attempt to include psychological concepts. When artistic works are unstructured, they hit harder and penetrate deeper. An attempt to formalize them, adding to their sophistication by absorbing psychology python-like, only succeeeds in detracting from their effectiveness and universality.

Writing in 1889, Strindberg might have spoken for the mid-twentieth century when he said, "Psychological processes are what interest the people of our own day more than anything else. Our souls, so eager for knowledge, cannot rest satisfied with seeing what happens, but must also learn how it comes to happen. We want to see the wires themselves, to watch the machinery."

Some of Strindberg's less successful but nevertheless

fascinating prose works written under Nietzsche's influence provide additional information about his developing psychosis. Later, after Nietzsche had become famous, Strindberg claimed that he had anticipated the idea of the Superman. Actually, he borrowed the Superman concept, using it in his novels "Tschandala" and "On the Seaboard."

Personal mayhem again formed the subject matter of "Tschandala," finished in 1888 at the height of his passion for Nietzsche. Strindberg was living near Copenhagen in a ruined castle, reading Poe's tales of the supernatural. Believing that his wife had tried to poison him, he consulted a psychiatrist to prove his sanity, then shifted his suspicions to a gypsy whom he accused of stealing his scientific secrets. The gypsy, a caretaker of the castle, retaliated by accusing Strindberg of cohabiting with his daughter and started blackmailing him. All of these fantastic events are used in "Tschandala," in which Strindberg portrays himself as a superior being, able to destroy the gypsy by using suggestion and black magic. The Superman could vanquish his foes at a distance. Strindberg in his developing insanity began to feel that his evil thoughts could be used magically to eliminate his enemies. He informed his friend George Brandes of these new powers, offering to rid Brandes of his enemies by sticking pins into their effigies. In primitive tribes this might be considered superstition; for the scientifically-minded Strindberg, it was evidence of insanity. Later he felt responsible for causing the deaths of many famous people by merely wishing them dead.

What would happen if a Superman actually existed, practicing the theories Nietzsche preached? Strindberg said later that he had attempted to embody the Superman directly in his novel "On The Seaboard" (1890). He did not think that the world was ready for a Zarathustra, and he showed in the novel how the Superman was destined to be misunderstood and destroyed by the inferiors who surround him. A man could be bold in judgment, quick in execution, the possessor of all Christian and pagan virtues and still perish. Survival of the fittest did not mean triumph of the most sensitive. Even the Superman had an Achilles heel—women would be his undoing and insanity his fate, just as they were Strindberg's.

The hero of "On the Seaboard" arrives in Strindberg's favorite locale, the Stockholm islands. Sensitive, haughty and disdainful of those who do not obey his orders when he speaks ex cathedra, Axel Borg quickly engenders antipathy among his neighbors. He scoffs at the Almighty when warned by a minister that his atheism and pride will call down God's revenge. Gradually, like Strindberg himself, he becomes more and more isolated, filled with a boundless scorn for humanity. Sleep becomes difficult; increasing anxiety is again compared to an electric current passing through the nerves. Paranoid feelings develop—"the mania of persecution was the first symptom of that infirmity which accompanies isolation." Borg meets a woman who can save him, but his uncompromising demands that she be completely subservient lead instead to her becoming faithless, like all women.

The final section of "On The Seaboard," written five years before Strindberg's own acute psychotic breakdown, contains a magnificent description of the disintegration accompanying a schizophrenic illness. Borg, formerly an immaculate and orderly man, now goes about unkempt and sloppily dressed, disinterested in his environment. When he becomes completely insane, he believes that only his departed mother can save him. "But the memory of his dead mother began to come up, and he awoke often from dreaming that he had lain as a child on her breast. His soul was plainly in retrogression, and the memory of the mother, the source, the link between conscious and unconscious life, the consoler, the interceder, came forth. Childhood thoughts of meeting again in another world come up, and his first plan of suicide expressed itself as an irresistible longing to find again his mother somewhere in another world which he did not believe in."

Strindberg always recognized the weakness concealed by the grandiose feelings he and Nietzsche shared. There was a reason for wanting to feel all powerful—it helped to hide the emptiness, fear, and longing that lay beneath. This perception was never used in the naturalistic drama Strindberg and Nietzsche founded. But with complete honesty Strindberg admitted to himself what he denied to others—he was a weak, mentally unbalanced man in danger of complete collapse. He still believed in the possibility that another woman might save him. The only woman who really mattered could never return.

CHAPTER FIVE

PRELUDE *to* PANIC

"Placed between two alternatives, either to kill a woman or be killed by her, I took a third one—I left her, and my first marriage was dissolved." On April 1, 1889, Strindberg returned alone to Sweden.

Denied the emotional support of the wife he needed so desperately, it is amazing that his personality remained relatively intact for another five years. However, the interval between the separation and Strindberg's acute schizophrenic illness was a period of gradual flight from reason. The progress of his mental illness had thus far been slow. We have seen the nascent fears of insanity and loss of control while he was a university student in Uppsala. When Strindberg was twenty-six and courting his wife, he referred to madness for the second time, coming to the conclusion that he was sometimes subject to mental delusions. Afterwards, he said that he possessed "the cunning of a madman," skillfully using his developing illness to obtain the affection that prevented further disintegration. There is much evidence to support Karl Jaspers, who dates the onset of Strindberg's schizophrenic illness to the early 1880's. We are fortunate in having an eyewitness picture of Strindberg early in 1880, when he arrived in Paris to pursue some research. Two of his closest and most tolerant friends were the famous Norwegian authors

Jonas Lie and B. Bjornson. They described being with Strindberg in a bank where a teller asked, routinely, to see his passport. Strindberg became violently suspicious, stating that he was being trapped because his radical views were known in Paris, and he identified King Oscar II of Sweden as the leader of the plot against him. In a letter to Jonas Lie, he diagrammed how a bomb might be placed under the throne in the Stockholm Royal Palace to destroy his enemy, but he decided to give up the plan in preference "to smash my enemies with bombs out of my ink bottle."

In the years that followed, Strindberg's family and friends tried desperately to sustain his reason. He often succeeded in his attempts to excite compassion in others, and those who respected his talents refused to abandon him to madness. It was evident as early as 1880 that his feelings of persecution were not limited to his wife and a female plot. As his paranoia worsened, his closest friends were included in the expanding list of enemies. For thirteen years Strindberg's wife Siri, admittedly no paragon of female virtues, bore the brunt of his accusations, serving as "keeper," mother of his children, and subject of his finest plays. Strindberg's eldest daughter, Karin, has described her mother's courage during the last years of the marriage, living under the threat of murder while she tried desperately to save her husband.

Just prior to the separation, Strindberg began to suffer from a psychotic thought disorder. The incident of Ibsen and "The Wild Duck" has already been mentioned. In 1888, after reading the works of Poe, Strindberg started to think that the dead could influence the living. He shared many of Poe's ideas and a large amount of his psychopathology. Strindberg's new hero also idolized the Virgin Mother, and liked his bottle of absinthe. Poe was interested in occult science and mental telepathy, and had a necrophilic fascination with death. Poe himself died in 1849, the year Strindberg was born. When Strindberg discovered this fact, he soon developed the firm belief that Poe's spirit had been reincarnated into his body, and that Poe's genius had been transferred to his brain by vibration. This idea became so fixed that he failed to check the dates; had he done so, he would have found that Poe died ten months after he was born. When reality is distorted by a thinking disorder, the victim never bothers to verify details. At first glance, these ideas of influence received from Poe might be attributed to increased suggestibility. The fact that they represented more serious illness was proven by later developments. Initially Strindberg felt that other people could influence his thoughts. Later he believed that he could control others and read their minds through his power of mental telepathy. It was part of a gradual transition to a terrifying stage during Strindberg's psychosis, when he was frightened by his imagined power to do evil to his loved ones by thinking evil thoughts.

After six years of wandering in Europe, Strindberg spent his first summer on the Stockholm islands, where nature once again soothed his suspicions. The renewal of life in the Swedish landscape made him feel that, no matter how bleak the past, the future gave promise of better times. In gratitude, he gathered material for a book on Swedish flora. The next winter Strindberg wrote and suffered in solitude, fighting to forget his feelings of persecution. One thing became clear—he needed female companionship. In the spring of 1890 he went to the Archipelago for a short reunion with his wife and children. Apart from Siri he was unhappy, but together with her life was a nightmare. In 1891 came the divorce proceedings, filled with rancor. Unpublished letters indicate that during the divorce trial Strindberg had the delusion that people had accused him of having venereal disease.

The notoriety of the divorce made him famous in the press, but closed the publishing houses to his books. With alimony to pay, Strindberg was soon without funds and pursued by creditors. Neglect by the Swedish literary world seemed like further persecution; later he was to identify himself with Christ as a fellow sufferer denied the respect of his countrymen. However, on the Continent respect for his work continued to grow, and Strindberg decided to emigrate again.

Desperate people try many outlets for relief. One of the illusions preserved by the paranoid individual is that a change of locale may cause his bothersome ideas of persecution to disappear. Unfortunately, this maneuver rarely works—Strindberg had tried it eight years previously without success. While in Denmark he had been befriended by the Swedish writer Ola Hansson and his wife, with whom he continued to correspond. Strindberg's plight now sounded so desperate from his letters that Mrs. Hansson wrote to a newspaper requesting a subscription to provide funds for him to leave Sweden. In 1892 he left Stockholm and came to live with the Hanssons.

Feelings of gratitude did not prevent his ideas of persecution from returning with new fury. Kindly interest was mistaken for evil intent. Soon Mrs. Hansson, who mothered him, seemed too solicitous—she must think that he is crazy. Perhaps she was another one of the women in the plot, seeking to gain control over him, suck out his life blood, steal his potency. Mrs. Hansson was friendly with Nietzsche's sister, and began urging Strindberg to publish his Nietzsche letters to capitalize on Nietzsche's new fame. We have seen how Strindberg was frightened lest these letters be used as evidence to commit him to an asylum. Was Mrs. Hansson conspiring with his wife to put him away? One day he accompanied the Hanssons and a doctor friend on a visit to a nearby hospital. He became terrified that the visit was a ruse to whisk him away quietly to the asylum.

The Hanssons were sincere friends, aiding Strindberg in his escape from a hostile Sweden, encouraging and assisting him to produce his plays in Berlin, where he had a more sympathetic audience. But by now Strindberg was suspicious of everyone, and had included all of his friends among his persecutors. No one could even approach him without incurring suspicion. If friends accepted his entreaties for money and support, he became suspicious of ulterior motives. If they refused, he considered his suspicions validated—they had been against him all along.

Strindberg's tenuous hold on sanity remained in his desperate hunger for human companionship. In Berlin, having turned away his more stable close friends, he frequented the company of drifting bohemians, where the obligations of friendship were few. The Berlin drifters of the 1890's were of a much higher class than their modern beatnik counterparts. Men like the outstanding Norwegian painter and future schizophrenic Edvard Munch, the brilliant writer and future Nobel prize winner Knut Hamsun, the alcoholic Polish poet Stanislav Przybyszewski, and the physician Carl Schleich were members of the bistro group Strindberg joined. The celebration of their collective despair and unrequited hunger for fame was their chief preoccupation, as it was to be in the similarly talented and mentally disturbed Parisian group of the 1920's.

Although he felt desolate, Strindberg quickly became disenchanted with this type of existence. It was true that alcohol helped him to dissolve the guilt he felt on deserting his children, and enabled him, as in adolescence, to engage in fleeting sexual affairs. But sin obsessed him when he awoke from the debaucheries of the night. In 1896, while acutely psychotic, he felt that he was in Hell. Now, in a shadowy tavern (christened "The Black Pig"), he felt that he was in an antechamber of Hell and that his fellow carousers were inspired by the Devil.

This period was crucial in the final development of Strindberg's delusions of persecution. The alcoholic Polish poet Przybyszewski, a mystic who dabbled in all the sexual perversions, attached himself closely to Strindberg. When Strindberg entered the tavern, Przybyszewski would greet him as his father and cover his hands with kisses. Once he offered Strindberg the key to his apartment, inviting him to sleep with his mistress. This girl, referred to by the exotic name Aspasia, took turns cohabiting with various members of the literary circle. Munch, Przybyszewski, and Strindberg enjoyed her favors, and after Strindberg had left Berlin, Przybyszewski deserted his family to marry her. During Strindberg's acute psychosis his main delusion was that Przybyszewski had followed him to Paris to kill him in revenge for his having had sexual relations with Aspasia.

The strong homosexual overtones to Strindberg's relationship with Przybyszewski again raise the question of the link between homosexuality and feelings of persecution. According to Sprigge's biography, homosexuality was prevalent in Strindberg's Berlin group. Although there is little doubt that Przybyszewski had a strong homosexual attachment to Strindberg, there is no evidence that Strindberg ever indulged in homosexual relations with Przybyszewski or anyone else. Freud has told us that it is the man with unconscious homosexual wishes who later develops feelings of persecution to deny their troublesome presence. Perhaps this was true with Strindberg, but when one enters the realm of speculation, reality begins blending with fantasy in the mind of the psychologist much as it does in the disordered mind of his subject. Suffice it to say that once again in Strindberg's illness, as in most paranoid illness, homosexual content is present without any firm evidence that it is the causative factor.

The more Strindberg became involved in this life of careless abandon, the less peace he obtained. Nights of revelry failed to drive away his growing feelings of guilt, and in the haze of morning hangovers, his children obsessed him. Strindberg once said that only a man felt true maternal love. Children were the link of marriage—the tragedy of divorce affected them more than adults who had time to become accustomed to the world's callousness. The poem "Laokoon'" and the play "Facing Death" repeated the principal theme of this period in his life—a father dying to redeem his children, asking no mercy for himself. Strindberg distributed pictures of his children to whoever would listen sympathetically while he moaned about their fate.

One of the recipients who was captivated by the photo of his little boy was a young Austrian girl of high birth named Freda Uhl. Having ambitions to be a writer, she met Strindberg while slumming among the bohemians to gather material. Strindberg was again desperate for female attention. He was beginning to feel that only another marriage with an unspoiled woman would help him find a haven and allay his suspicions. Freda puzzled and haunted him. Being twenty-four years younger than he, she had an aura of innocence, yet she was changeable and vital. Again the mercurial type of woman attracted him, rather than the steady, accepting hausfrau that he needed. This time, however, he came closer to complementing himself, for Freda had Latin traits as well as Nordic. Often sloppy and childish, she became at times the ultra-practical woman of the world, alternating between soothing and commanding. Unfortunately, like Siri, she had an attraction to the stage and veiled intentions of using Strindberg's talent to further her own ambition.

Freda Uhl left a record of her years with Strindberg, titled "Marriage With Genius." Written four decades later, it is dripping with romanticism and suitable for popular magazines. For example, here is the first reference to Strindberg—"You were chosen and doomed to be a prophet. But I witnessed your martyrdom. You saw what others did not see and heard what others did not hear. You overcame time and space—" etc., etc. Freda felt that Strindberg fulfilled a need in her life. She saw herself as Senta in Wagner's *The Flying Dutchman,* redeeming Strindberg from his curse by her self-sacrifice. Why, Strindberg even wore a Flying Dutchman cape, and he certainly seemed to be a wanderer in search of a woman; perhaps if he found a woman with love faithful in the face of death he could be redeemed from the curse laid on him by the Devil. If this seems far-fetched, Freda confirms it when she writes of Strindberg, "A home! Would not a home be redemption for the Flying Dutchman?" This fantasy coincided with Strindberg's needs; later he wrote in "The Road to Damascus," "It was my dream, you know, to seek redemption through a woman."

She pursued him steadily, displaying her charms and her talent as a potential savior, until Strindberg succumbed and proposed, writing, "Now the man lays his head in your lap as a sign that the good in you overcomes the evil in him, but do not misuse your power." Sick as he was, Strindberg saw the ominous signs in a marriage with a young ambitious woman. What would she save him for? By now his interest in mental telepathy had solidified into the belief that his evil thoughts could destroy his enemies, and he had already started chemical experiments in an effort to manufacture gold. After one farewell debauch, Strindberg fell physically ill, and Freda forgave his transgression, nursing him, with flowers at his bedside, as Siri had nursed him many years before. Perhaps she had been sent as a redeemer—she gave him a breath of lost youth, and this swayed what little remained of his judgment.

So, despite opposition from the bride's family, Strindberg and Freda Uhl were betrothed. His prospective sister-in-law, a stable girl with considerable psychological acumen, has left letters describing Strindberg during this period—"He doesn't understand fun, rarely jokes, continually believes himself persecuted and despised. . . . I can never shake off the fear of seeing him suddenly go insane. At the same time he more and more impresses me as a great genius."

Shortly after the marriage, Strindberg began to feel that he was being controlled by "the powers." Fearful that his past would reveal his dark secrets, he forbade his wife to obtain "The Confession of a Fool," saying, "Don't read it; you will poison yourself." After she had disobeyed him she found herself accused of the same persecutions as Siri. Strindberg suspected his new wife of spying on him, reading his mail, and acting as his keeper and jailer. When he felt certain that she could read his thoughts, murderous impulses appeared. Once more he tried a change of locale in an effort to fight these destructive feelings of persecution. The couple left on a trip to England.

Strindberg had been invited to visit England by his publishers, to provide further publicity for his widely known books. Freda was ecstatic at the prospect of increasing her own and her husband's fame in the English-speaking countries. But her enthusiasm was soon cooled by Strindberg's insane behavior. At Gravesend he felt for the first time that he was being persecuted by an electrical machine, and went searching for the machine in the attic and behind closed doors. Sulphur fumes filled every room in which they stayed. Strindberg had brought along his chemical apparatus so as to lose no precious time in deciphering nature's secrets by converting sulphur into gold. In London, his mental state deteriorated still further, and he suppressed an impulse to push Freda into the Thames. Standing on London Bridge, he suddenly felt terrified by a vision of a group of East End denizens who appeared to be closing in on him.

The prelude to panic was beginning. Strindberg fled from his wife, accusing her of hating him because he was a man. In Hamburg he had an attack of agoraphobia in the open street during rush hour, remaining motionless out of fear of his hostile surroundings. A friend, Adolf Paul, spirited him off to the Danish island of Rügen, where he spent the hot summer of 1893 in seclusion, conducting his chemical experiments. The feeling that he was in Hell, tortured like the poor wretches in Dante's *Inferno,* soon descended on him again. Freda had corresponded with his friend Paul—for him this proved that Paul was joining the plot. Strindberg left quickly for his mother-in-law's home in Odense, Denmark, where he felt again that he was being watched and that Satan was leading him into a nest of snakes. Precipitating one crisis after another, he was finally thrown out by his relatives and fled back to a furnished room in Berlin.

By the winter of 1893-94 Strindberg was wandering in a daze. In the past, even when suffering greatly, he was able to continue working. Now, with his thinking disorder worsened, he could no longer write creatively. Instead, a

fantastic idea suddenly possessed him. Perhaps plants were
descended from animals, and had a nervous system that
had escaped scientific detection. This peculiar idea could
be tested by seeing if plants were sensitive to morphine.
Strindberg assembled an injecting kit and roamed the
countryside injecting the local flora, looking for human
responses in their leaves. Near a mental colony he was
accosted by a farmer while he was injecting morphine
into the twig of an apple tree, and was accused of being
an escaped lunatic. Later, he published the results of his
researches in a short pamphlet, "Have Plants Nerves?"
This document is a perfect example of schizophrenic
writing with its illogical rambling from topic to topic and
its loosening of associations. It is fascinating to read how
the disordered mind connects past and present. After a
confused discussion of animals that convert themselves
into plants, and the claim that plants possess nerves because they are descended from animals, Strindberg refers
to the sex organs of plants, especially mistletoe. Seven
years previously, while writing "The Growth of a Soul,"
he had compared himself to mistletoe, the plant that always needed support. Now he writes, "The Mistletoe,
which at first had to creep up trees, has in the sequel
become completely a parasite." The pamphlet concludes
with a comparison of plants with the organs of animals.
The tubes of climbing plants are a degenerated spinal
cord, the leaves are skin, and so on. Such illogical thinking is universally typical of the written productions of
hospitalized schizophrenics.

Freda rejoined Strindberg in Berlin during the winter
for still another attempt to save him, and soon found herself pregnant. This was unfortunate, for, as previously
noted, Strindberg's feelings of persecution markedly diminished whenever his wives expected children. The tem-

porarily serene couple then journeyed to Austria to await the coming of the baby at Freda's family home. Safe in his mother-in-law's house, Strindberg increased the tempo of his researches into the occult. In the evenings he experimented with a secret process of photographing the moon. By day he continued his burning of sulphur in futile attempts to make gold, sending samples off for chemical analysis. A real persecution intensified his illness still further. After the publication of "The Confession of a Fool" in Germany, he was arrested on a charge of immorality. This strained relations with his Catholic in-laws, and brought a painful reminder to his wife of the fate of Siri Von Essen. Strindberg once more became terrified that his enemies were pursuing him.

After the baby's arrival, Freda's peaceful interlude was over. Strindberg accused her of reading his mail and being in league with the enemies who were attempting to steal his scientific secrets. His growing, uncontrollable hostility toward the family and neighbors provoked retaliation. A local witch hunter attributed the baby's ceaseless crying to a punishment for Strindberg's atheism. As the sulphur fumes rose from the chimney, a neighborhood Bernadette saw a vision of the Devil in the backyard. Strindberg's presence in any household seemed to disturb domestic tranquillity. Again he prepared to move on. If only he could score a great scientific triumph, all of his eccentric behavior would be vindicated. Desperately he sent off samples of "intermediate gold" to Berlin for analysis. When he failed again to convince the world of his imagined scientific genius, he became more paranoid. Once more Strindberg searched for a doctor who would testify to his sanity. Letters to his friends were written in gibberish, indicating the severity of his thinking disorder. Referring to his marriage he wrote, "All women hate

Buddhas, maltreat, disturb, humiliate, annoy them, with
the hatred of inferiors, because they themselves can never
become Buddhas.—English physicians have recently established that when two children of a family sleep in the
same bed, the weaker draws strength from the stronger.
There you have marriage: the brother and sister bed."

Even as Strindberg approached the nadir of schizophrenic panic, his push toward mental health can be observed in another statement he made: "I dream of days
gone by, and have a longing to fly in some warmish
medium, neither air nor water—to have no more enemies,
neither to hate nor be hated any more." Now that Freda
was reading his mind and had joined his enemies, all hope
for redemption through a woman had vanished. Feeling
pursued, Strindberg fled alone from Austria and sought
sanctuary in Paris, where he continued his chemical experiments. This new voyage of the Flying Dutchman
made him seem more romantic, and Freda followed him
to Paris, where fresh hostilities ensued. In November,
1894, the illness of her other child summoned Freda back
to Austria, never to see her husband again.

Strindberg felt overjoyed at her leaving. Describing the
closing days of his second marriage in "Fair Haven and
Foul Strand," he said he had "an indistinct suspicion that
life had no complete reality, but was a dream stage, and
that our actions, even the worst of them, were carried out
under the influence of some strong suggestive power other
than ourselves." This same unknown power seemed to
destine him for a higher purpose. Strindberg felt as if he
were soaring, ascending to a new psychotic reality where
his pain would be alleviated and where he hoped to find
peace.

CHAPTER SIX

The PANIC *of* INSANITY

When Jesus made love the paramount force of his teachings, he may not have been absolutely right, but that love
does help in times of stress few would dispute. Strindberg's
"Inferno" begins with a decision to abandon love.
"Obliged to choose between love and knowledge, I had
decided to strive for the highest knowledge," he tells us
at the commencement of his acute schizophrenic illness.

During the years of developing persecution we have
seen how much Strindberg relied on the love and devotion
of others to support his self-esteem. While he had a wife
or other people deeply interested in him, he maintained
his weak contact with reality. The relationships with his
wives were obviously disturbed, but sick relationships are
better than no relationships at all. Deprived of these
human contacts, Strindberg's illness had to worsen. When
these props were removed, only increasing grandiose feelings from within could sustain him. With convenient
rationalization, the paranoid individual justifies his symptoms in the light of his exalted opinion of himself. He
begins to feel that he must really be important, else why
should people go to the trouble of persecuting him? Later,
even common mortals will not suffice as persecutors—
gradually sufferings are attributed to the might of unknown powers. Imagining himself on this pinnacle of per-

secution, Strindberg made himself inaccessible to ordinary people like his family and friends, saying, "I am surrounded by silence and loneliness."

The loneliness suffered by Strindberg approached, but never quite reached, the "end-of-the-world" feeling suffered by many schizophrenics, and picturesquely described in the Schreber memoirs. It had a touch of the "ivory tower" type of loneliness first made fashionable by Alfred de Vigny. Before Strindberg became ill, he always idolized the eventual martyrdom of the man of creative talent, adhering to the theory that creative artists must produce original work alone and in suffering. In the "Blue Book" he wrote, "A real poet must sacrifice his person for his work." The solitary nature of genius is not necessarily connected with illness; however, when illness supervenes, it may impede recovery.

Actually, Strindberg retained anchors in sanity even during his wildest insane excursions. Never completely withdrawing from outside activities, he visited bookshops, laboratories, and the Sorbonne to converse with people about his occult scientific interests. The exaggerated scientific curiosity which provided the framework for his psychotic withdrawal also maintained contact with his previous personality. We have noted how Strindberg had been fascinated by experiments in chemistry and electricity since childhood. In adult life he had studied medicine in a further effort to divine the secrets of nature. Each spring the magical changing of the season excited his curiosity, leading him to botanical explorations in the Stockholm islands and on the Continent. Without this background in rational scientific knowledge, it is probable that Strindberg's schizophrenic preoccupations would have remained fixed and unquestioned. Instead, his continuous efforts to understand himself and the structure of the physical world aided his struggle for recovery.

Alone in Paris, almost from the beginning Strindberg realized that if he could bring himself to trust people he would recover. Soon it was Christmas, more important to the Swedes as a family festival than for its religious aspects. Fighting his suspicions with the good will of the season, Strindberg accepted a dinner invitation from a Scandinavian family. But the sight of others happily engaged in Yuletide festivities while he was burning with hatred proved unendurable; he fled into the December night, reminded of his desertion of his children, thirsting for revenge against the world that had made him an outcast.

Revenge for a schizophrenic may assume many forms. Hatred may be subtly vented in interpersonal relationships or suddenly discharged in antisocial acts. Strindberg's chemical experiments provided an outlet for his tremendous hostility toward all who surrounded him. Later, in "The Road to Damascus" he revealed the purpose behind these experiments in medieval alchemy. First, making gold helped feed his feelings of grandiosity—he would be "a man who has done what no one else has ever done; who will overthrow the Golden Calf and upset the tables of the money changers. I will hold the fate of the world in my crucible." Second, and most important, the manufacture of gold was intended not for accumulating wealth, but as a calculated act of destruction. "I'll do it (make gold) to paralyze the present order," Strindberg tells us, "to disrupt it as you'll see. I am the destroyer, the dissolver, the world incendiary; and when all lies in ashes, I shall wander hungrily through the heaps of ruins, rejoicing at the thought that it is all my work: that I have written the last page of world history, which can then be held to be ended."

Working furiously in his furnished room to fulfill these hostile ambitions, Strindberg seemed to show a decreased awareness of sensory stimuli and a lack of concern about

his personal habits. It is almost as if concern with his delusions had become pre-eminent, blotting out external sensation. While heating a crucible of sulphur in an attempt
to make gold, he severely burned his hands. Ordinarily
fastidious about his personal appearance and hypersensitive to even the slightest physical injury, Strindberg now
ignored the charred flesh and was oblivious to the pain.
Soon he was prostrate with blood poisoning and was admitted to the Hospital of St. Louis.

The scenes in the hospital were replete with meaning
for the future development of Strindberg's symptoms.
When people are physically ill, they often regress to patterns of childhood dependency. Strindberg, so desperate
for the love he had abandoned, demonstrated this strik-
ingly in the description of the care he received—"They
dress me and undress me, and look after me like a child.
The kind sister takes a fancy to me and treats me like a
baby, calls me 'my child,' while I call her 'mother!'"
Already, in the beginning of his acute illness we see a
mixture of religion and mother. Suffering with religious
resignation was one of the virtues taught him by his
Pietistic mother, although not accepted by him at the
time. Pietism had been presented to him "as a kind of
European Buddhism, regarding the world as an unclean
place of punishment for the soul." Now the hospital nuns
"taught him the joys of suffering, for they know the bene-
ficial effects of pain."

In his constant mingling of childhood fantasy and adult
reality, Strindberg recapitulated hostile feelings toward
his mother, while commenting on the sister who nursed
him—"The old lady, an Augustine Nun, wears the garb
of the dead because she has never lived." Yet the motherly
atmosphere at this Catholic hospital started the recovery
process in motion even before the persecutions had

reached their height. Strindberg's return to religion during the recovery period in a sense represented a reunion with the Pietistic mother of his childhood. This was especially true since in personal life he had failed to find the maternal woman he craved. Religious feeling, and the distant memories it evoked, provided satisfaction during the illness, when he gave up the search for a real woman as futile. Once more, as in childhood, woman could only be visualized as a religious chimera, because as such she was asexual like the Virgin Mary. As Strindberg lapsed deeper into his pyschosis, this view of women as asexual beings became fixed, just as children must always view their parents as the pure sexless upholders of all Christian virtues.

The extent of Strindberg's understanding of his illness while he was in the midst of turmoil is truly fantastic. As he leaves the hospital, he recognizes that in the religious tie to his mother lies the strength which will lead him to eventual recovery. Strindberg writes, "At parting I wish to kiss the hand of the faithful mother, who, without speaking many words has taught me the way of the Cross." The three institutions founded by St. Louis symbolize what his illness will mean to him—St. Louis Hospital, the Sorbonne, the Church of Saint Chapelle—"From suffering, through knowledge, to repentance."

Encouraged by the tender care received from the sisters in the hospital, Strindberg returns to the solitude of his room, where the soothing effects soon wear off. It is winter. Continuing the confused pursuit of alchemy with caldrons of burning sulphur, he prepares for future suffering. Now he believes that the secrets of creation will soon be revealed to him. Strindberg feels himself in a new world, where the traditional methods of communication with his fellow mortals seem unnecessary and inconsequential. As he soars into the emancipated world of the psychotic, past frustrations are forgotten. He feels unbridled strength, the ability to perform miracles. Powerless and inadequate in his former social relationships, impatient in his desire to inflict pain on his insensitive detractors, Strindberg now feels able to exert evil telepathic influence on absent friends. Like Nietzsche, he realizes that the desire to injure others has arisen from his own frightful loneliness.

It is February, 1896. A plot is slowly forming in the hotel—pianos are played to annoy him—nails are hammered over his bed. He begins to feel that he must be handed over to Satan to be tried before God informs him of his special mission. In a desperate search for understanding, he consults the Book of Job to find the reason for his sufferings. The first flight of the schizophrenic panic takes place—Strindberg moves to a hotel for Catholic students, where there is a picture of St. Peter above his bed.

To describe the weird occurrences of the winter of 1896, Strindberg resorts to direct quotations from his diary. Miraculous things happen during the alchemy experiments. Strange sulphurous shapes remind him of people both hated and feared. The conspiracy forms further, and diabolical significance is attributed to innocent happenings. As spring approaches, the idea that he has the power to influence others by mental telepathy seems confirmed; his children fall ill in Sweden, and he believes that his attempts at magic have caused this misfortune.

It is the Sunday before Easter and Strindberg is obsessed with the mystical significance of death and resurrection. Wandering on the quays he purchases a copy of Balzac's novel "Seraphita," and is reintroduced to his brilliant psychotic countryman, Swedenborg. As usual, the paranoid schizophrenic must provide a logical meaning for external events that others consider insignificant. Strindberg believes that this chance reading of "Seraphita" is part of the powers' plan to prepare him for a higher existence—"I felt like a perfectly righteous man whom the Eternal was testing, and whom the purgatory of this world would soon make fit for deliverance." Misinterpretations of reality, attributed to the intervention of the powers, follow in quick succession. Female statues remind him of his wife. Numbers on scraps of paper have occult meaning. A cushion on which he rests assumes the appearance of a marble head. Dreams warn Strindberg against hidden dangers, dreams similar to Swedenborg's at the beginning of his schizophrenic illness.

There must be an avenger if he has to undergo all these persecutions in preparation for his special mission. The schizophrenic's imaginary persecutors often crystallize into a single person or a small group. Strindberg's persecutory delusions developed in a fascinating way. In the early stage, while writing "The Father" and "The Confession of a Fool," he felt that his wife was persecuting him and trying to drive him insane. Closer inspection revealed that all women possessed personality characteristics similar to his wife's—it was a universal trait for a woman to be a vampire, sucking man's strength. Then Strindberg turned his attention to the question—Why he? Whom had he injured to be placed in the unique situation of being persecuted? With the religious fervor of his adolescence, Strindberg considered the answer in terms of sin—what sin had he committed? The answer gradually became evident. He had absconded with another man's wife. True, he was not wholly to blame; as he portrays in "The Confession of a Fool," his rival acquiesced, practically inviting Strindberg to take her, and she pursued and seduced him despite his attempts to break away. But this did not matter. In fact, it made the situation worse. He had still stolen another man's wife, and sought punishment for this sin. By 1889, when he wrote the play "Creditors," this idea had taken full possession of his mind. In "Creditors" the cuckold returns to conspire with his wife. His former rival has remained a creditor, determined to avenge himself by driving Strindberg insane. The strange power the persecuting husband possesses is compared to the current of an electric generator.

Contrary to expectations, it was the alcoholic Polish poet Stanislav Przybyszewski, not the wronged husband, who became Strindberg's main persecutor during his acute schizophrenic illness. The reason for this change becomes clear when we recall similarities in his relationship with Przybyszewski. After his departure from Sweden, Strindberg settled in Berlin, where he met Przybyszewski and participated in the activities of a bohemian group. Here he cohabited with a Scandinavian girl called Aspasia, who was also the mistress of Przybyszewski. Like the previous cuckold, Przybyszewski was very accommodating—in fact he offered Strindberg the key to his apartment, almost inviting him to sleep with Aspasia. Then Strindberg married, separated, and fled to Paris. In the interim, Przybyszewski deserted his legal wife and children to marry Aspasia. Strindberg believed that Przybyszewski had become his chief persecutor, seeking him in Paris, planning to kill him in revenge for having had sexual relations with Aspasia.

Strindberg awaits execution with a feeling of anger and remorse, for he feels that death alone can deliver him from the pangs of his conscience. During May and June of 1896, the piano-playing resumes, and horrible dreams and strange occurrences continue. He feels the Voltaire bridge sway under his feet. A paperweight of the Madonna of Lourdes develops into an imaginary head of Christ. June 18, 1896—Strindberg learns that Przybyszewski has been arrested in Vienna on a charge of murdering his former wife and children. The misfortune of his imagined persecutor, far from alleviating his fears, intensifies the symptoms. He blames himself for the crime, and the subsequent release of Przybyszewski for lack of evidence fails to mollify his guilt. Death seems inevitable. He makes one last Herculean effort to convert sulphur to gold. Failing, he seeks solace in prayer and the Bible.

Strindberg now enters a stage of his illness in which hallucinations and delusions are the most prominent feature. Many schizophrenics go through years of illness without these secondary symptoms of the disease; when they do occur, as in Strindberg's case, they may make a fleeting and terrifying appearance. Strindberg begins to hear voices. He feels a strange magnetic fluid streaming from the walls of the room. These phenomena indicate to him that his persecutor is discharging a stream of gas through the wall in an effort to kill him. He resists the impulse to request police protection, fearing that the police will take him to a lunatic asylum. (Here and subsequently, Strindberg's insight into the possibility that he might be mad prevents him from saying and doing things which would have resulted in enforced hospitalization.) Since the gas fails, Strindberg now believes that Przybyszewski will try to electrocute him. His enemy is enlisting the assistance of others—he quarrels with neighbors, and suspects the night porter of aiding in the construction of an electrical machine. To foil the persecutors he changes his room, but —strips of metal are being stored in the next room, hammering is heard over his bed—the construction of the infernal persecuting machine continues. Perhaps it is all his imagination, but the persecution seems so real! Even during Sundays, the days of religious renewal, he is in Hell. Even nature now fails to dissipate his suffering.

July 14, 1896—Judgment night arrives. From an unknown source Strindberg learns that the machine has been completed. Remembering that his mother had told him of the disgrace of dirty feet on such occasions, he cleanses his body, reads the Psalms, and prepares for the tortures and death of the night. The clock strikes two. He feels as if an air pump has been applied to his heart, and the electric stream strikes him to the marrow. He rushes terrified out of the room, again seeking relief in the garden, where he falls into a tranquil sleep to be awakened by the sun and the renaissance of the morn.

Again we must recall the fascinating continuity of these psychotic ideas with Strindberg's developing personality and feelings. As an adolescent, he had placed great emphasis on his experiments and his interest in electricity. In past periods of extreme anxiety he had felt that electricity was being passed through his body. These torments included events during the turmoil of his first marriage, the incident on the opening night of his first play, and an episode of terror while he was on a visit to England. Periods of creative activity were also associated with electrical sensations. Later, during the prelude to his illness, he equated electricity with hatred. When he hated people the animosity acted like a sponge, helping his enemies to succeed in their persecutions. Strindberg wrote, "My hatred became a conductor by which I received the currents of others." During his illness, he believed that when he could learn to turn the other cheek, the machine would cease operating. This struggle to achieve the spirit of Christian resignation was part of the perpetual battle Strindberg waged against his illness. He wanted to submit, reconciling himself to the fact that he was ill, but the attacks seemed so real. Had he not heard and seen the preparation of the persecuting machine? Yes, the persecutions were real, and only Divine Providence had saved him from death.

"In dealing with an enemy there are only two methods —either to kill him, or not to fight him but to fly," Strindberg tells us. Again he decided on flight. Perhaps his persecutors would not move such a heavy machine to a friend's home in Dieppe, where he now sought respite in an attic room. Unfortunately, as soon as he arrived, the feeling that he was being persecuted by electricity took renewed possession of him. After a scrupulous check of the surrounding rooms, he settled down for the night.

Describing his experiences in Dieppe, Strindberg gives a dramatic demonstration of a mentally ill person's constant desire to get well. In his bedroom, in the middle of the night, there occurs an amazing example of the schizophrenic's continuous testing of the reality of his perceptions in an effort to rid himself of the eroding distortions caused by the disease. Perhaps the electrical persecutions are part of his imagination and do not really exist. He will test for the presence of electric current by taking a compass to bed with him. He lights two candles. The clock strikes two. Strindberg reports: "Then I feel, at first only faintly, something like an inrush of electric fluid. I look at my compass, but it shows no sign of wavering. It is not electricity then. But the tension increases; my heart beats violently; I offer resistance, but as if by a flash of lightning my body is charged with a fluid which chokes me and depletes my blood. I rush down the stairs to the room on the ground floor, where they have made up for me a provisional bed in case of necessity. There I lie for five minutes and collect my thoughts. Is it radiating electricity? No;

for the compass has not been affected. Is it a diseased state of mind induced by fear of the fatal hour of two o'clock? No; for I have still the courage to defy attacks. But why must I light the candles and attract the mysterious fluid? In this labyrinth of questioning I find no answer, and try at last to go to sleep, but a new discharge of electricity strikes me like a cyclone, forces me to rise from bed, and the chase begins afresh. I hide myself behind the walls, lie down close to the doors, or in front of the stove. Everywhere, everywhere the furies find me. Overmastered by terror, I fly in panic from everything and nothing, from room to room, and finish by crouching down on the balcony."

Despite all of these efforts to avoid persecution, suffering brings a reality that logic cannot dispel. After a sleepless night, Strindberg realizes that he can no longer trust his own judgment. Realizing that he may be the victim of a nervous illness, he decides to return the next day to Sweden for medical treatment.

During the long voyage home, Strindberg's suspicions traveled with him like unwanted baggage. Yet, the fact that he sought treatment voluntarily augured well for eventual recovery. On arrival in Ystad in southern Sweden he is tormented again, suspecting his physician friend of inquiring about him prior to putting him away. His bed is an American fourposter, topped by four brass balls which look like the conductors of an electrical machine. The springs resemble induction coils. A wire net rolled over the bed must be an accumulator. After dark the persecutor feels for his heart to suck out his blood. Now the doctor is made part of the plot. Why? The doctor wants to do away with him after stealing his secret for making gold. Within a few days Strindberg becomes violently agitated, requiring sedation by cold water baths, one of the chief treatments for schizophrenia at that time and still a valuable adjunct to modern therapy.

The agitation was tranquillized, but the delusions continued unabated. America needed gold, and the doctor was offering the U. S. Government Strindberg's formula for its manufacture. To steal his secrets, the doctor is driving him mad with drugs, before finally poisoning him. Fearful of murder, Strindberg seeks other medical advice. His terror is so real that he is forced to blot many events from his memory, writing, "There occur in life such terrible incidents that the mind refuses to accept the memory of them for a moment, but the impression remains and becomes irresistibly alive again."

Strindberg was under medical treatment for one month before the tension became unbearable, forcing him to flee from the doctor's "torture chamber." As always, his feelings toward people were mixtures of tenderness and anger. He retained affection and gratitude toward his physician friend despite his suspicions. The doctor had given him support and encouragement which, raising his self-esteem, had made him feel better. However, it was a message from his family conveying their renewed and faithful love that allowed him to look kindly on the world again and seek the friendship of his executioners. The illness was beginning to abate. Real people like Przybyszewski were imagined as persecutors during the acute stage; now that Strindberg was able once more to accept human contacts, the plotting was attributed to "the powers." He felt the influence of "the powers" both before and after the acute illness, demonstrating again that schizophrenia is a chronic disease in which acute symptoms may be seen at short and infrequent intervals.

Recovery, always present in rudimentary form, began to progress more rapidly. It took the form of the recovery of

many schizophrenics of lesser intelligence who lack Strindberg's dialectical subtlety. Religion provided the matrix of
restitution. At first Strindberg's physician friend derogated
his great interest in religion, telling him that it was another
symptom of his illness. This was true; in fact nineteenth-
century psychologists believed that religious overexcitation
was a cause of a type of insanity termed religious mania.
But symptoms are often useful, acting as preservatives
against further deterioration. Religion may be an area of
compromise for the schizophrenic, through which psychotic symptoms can be partially resolved in a socially
acceptable framework. Sometimes this attempt at religious
resolution goes too far, ending in an identification with
Christ. Fleeting identifications with Christ are frequent—
their permanence often determines the eventual outcome
of the illness. If the patient, like Strindberg, feels an empathy with Christ as someone else who endured the ultimate in suffering, it is one thing; if he feels that he *is*
Christ, the Son of God, it is another. In the first case
religion provides an escape, in the second a quicksand.
The afflicted may become one with Christ in humility, or
unite with him in omnipotence. Empathizing with Christ
may indicate deep emotional resources, or be used to conceal an emptiness of feeling.

Strindberg looked upon Christ as a fellow sufferer, and
upon the Cross as his salvation. "Blessed is the man whom
the Lord chasteneth," he said, in a statement reflecting the
Pietism of his youth. Invited to see his infant daughter,
he drifts down the Danube, imagining her as the Beatrice
who will lead him to the Cross. The journey is difficult—
"Every hundred poles the Crucified meets me with his
crown of thorns and instills into me courage to bear
scourging and crucifixion." Strindberg feels like the penitent Faust, forgiven for his transgressions. With less in-

telligent schizophrenics the literary allusions are different, but the feelings are the same.

Mortification of the flesh became his ideal, again maintaining continuity with the adolescent Strindberg who eulogized martyrdom. Sensual love had been a curse. The sexless love of his little daughter and its reciprocation gave him the courage to continue his pilgrimage toward the distant City of God. Yet, much as Strindberg was helped by his communion with his two-and-a-half-year-old daughter, he still required someone of greater intellectual resources to serve as his mediator with the Almighty. Besides, his daughter was a Catholic, and it was anathema to him to make the sign of the Cross. He often said that, regardless of need, he could never deny the religion of his birth.

Strindberg's delusional thinking continued while his relatives attempted to convert him to Catholicism. Caught in a thunderstorm, he felt that it was a *deus ex machina* indicative of his power to control the elements. Finally his in-laws reintroduced him to Swedenborg, whom he immediately recognized as a fellow sufferer. Swedenborg's teachings neatly fitted in with Strindberg's delusions. Strindberg felt that he was in Hell, and believed that the powers had destined him for a higher purpose; Swedenborgian doctrine proclaimed suffering for past misdeeds, and the necessity of passage through Purgatory in preparation for a higher life. For a time the identification was complete—Swedenborg's Hell was identical with his own. Even the physiognomy of the Austrian countryside was the same. Finding peace in a rose room so beautifully described in "The Road to Damascus," Strindberg read Swedenborg's books continuously for eight days, commenting, "All my observations, feelings and thoughts are so vividly reflected there, that his visions seem to me like experiences and 'real' and human documents."

Unfortunately, the Swedenborgian experiences with which Strindberg empathized were also schizophrenic in content. Swedenborg, the fellow genius who restored Strindberg's self-respect, also believed in his ability to read the future and in his power of mental telepathy. Therefore, Strindberg's own ideas of influence were reinforced, and his evil thoughts continued to have strange effects and portents. In September, 1897, electrical phenomena returned, this time diminished in intensity and partially dissipated by his religious armor. The days of acute illness were less turbulent and he seemed to be building an immunity to personal attack. Once again Strindberg compulsively planned his creative work, as he did in former years. As the thinking disorder diminished, he was better able to use his perceptions, striving constantly to discover the purpose of his past suffering.

Perhaps, like Christ, he would be given special orders direct from God. During his religious restitution Strindberg came perilously close to this final identification with Christ, but fortunately he never reached it. Otherwise, he might have spent his remaining days in a mental hospital, and the brilliant works of his later years would never have been written. Once he pondered on the significance of his daughter's name, Christina. At times he felt certain that marks on his palms resembled large nail holes. During a renewal of his nightly torments he thought of the sufferings of Christ when soldiers spat in his face, buffeted him, and struck him with rods. Gradually Strindberg saw the differences between his own ordeal and Christ's. Christ suffered because of his righteousness; he must suffer as punishment for his sin. Men who were God's instruments had attempted to drive him mad for the sin of stealing another man's wife. The fact that fragments of his disjointed literary production were still printed provided some reassurance that his reason had not been grossly impaired. In gratitude Strindberg declared himself ready for full repentance.

Improvement in schizophrenic illness does not mean that the underlying disease process becomes absolutely quiescent. During recovery, attempts are made to cover the lacunae in personality structure left by the disease; this does not alter the disintegrating process that caused these gaps to develop. For example, even after recovery Strindberg retained belief in the reality of his persecutions, challenging psychiatrists to explain mystical occurrences without the intervention of the supernatural. Also, the feeling that his evil thoughts could cause others harm and sometimes death, never did disappear. Strindberg continued to be plagued by an alternation of feelings between grandiosity and insignificance. These oscillations were similar to the mercurial passions of his adolescent years, when his restless feelings seemed like the movements of an irregular pendulum. At one end he felt himself equal in power to the Lord, and a necessary instrument for God's revelation. At the other end contact with sanity remained, and he questioned his megalomania before retreating into insignificance. Slowly, Strindberg's conception of his place in the cosmos became more moderate. Two attributes aided him in achieving relative stability. First, there was religion, acting as a mantle to cover the defects in his personality. Second, his artistic sensitivity helped him find balance. The artist, with true aesthetic understanding of nature, comes to shun absolutes. Beneath his ebullient enthusiasm there lies hidden an adoration of the dynamic equilibrium in nature. While the artist seethes, unable to organize his own passions, he maintains a deep respect for the order in nature where he finds his inspiration. Once again Strindberg achieved stability during a periodic communion with nature, finding order in the presence of eternal change.

Strindberg said goodbye to the Danube with a typically Swedish comment—"I say to comfort myself, 'You were a dream, short as summer, too sweet to be real, and I do not regret it.' " The sojourn in Austria had served its purpose in leading him toward restitution, and as he left he compared himself to a restless pilgrim who had fought his way out of the caldron of Hell into the fires of Purgatory. Returning to Sweden, he settled in Lund, where he found people suffering from similar symptoms. Apparently others also dwelled in a Swedenborgian limbo called "Devastatio"—a place where sufferings were endured as part of a spiritual catharsis preparatory to salvation. With his flair for the histrionic, Strindberg began wearing a penitent's costume. Swedenborg had become his deliverer; he was the instrument of "the powers," leading him, not to the Catholicism of his in-laws, nor to the frigid Lutheranism of his countrymen, but to the compromise Pietism of his childhood. Many of his fellow countrymen seemed to require Swedenborg's guidance—Strindberg decided to forge his experience into words, providing religion in a new aspect for the spiritually needy and expectant multitude.

Not that these experiences were complete, or that he fully comprehended their significance. What was the aim of "the powers"? To Strindberg the same powers seemed to be operative throughout history. Dante, Swedenborg, and St. Paul were also affected by them—grandiosely he placed himself in élite company. Perhaps they supplied the vital force for the completion of the human type, the production of the higher man—"The Superman, as Nietzsche, that rod of chastisement, prematurely used and cast into the fire, has announced him." Could Strindberg, through the intervention of "the powers," become like the Nietzschean Superman?

At the sight of a lunatic asylum the pendulum quickly

swung back to humility. Nietzsche was in one, and Strindberg realized what he had escaped. Even if he believed he was a giant, he would have the tiresome job of convincing a doubting world. Besides, repentance was the only sure way to salvation. In searching for a method of purging his sin, Strindberg found himself in a quandary. Swedenborg was a valued leader, but his church sold its own brand of Christianity. Atonement was a continuous process. Why not unburden himself all at once by becoming a Catholic? A visit from a priest convinces him that adherence to the restrictions of the Catholic Church is not suitable for a man possessed of such grandiose desires for complete freedom. A newly converted friend suggests a rest in a Belgian convent. The idea of residing in a monastery fulfilled his desire for solitary contemplation and his need to perform good works as part of his repentance. It also appealed to a need to deny sexuality. While in Austria he had "dreamed again his old dream of a convent within whose walls he might be sheltered from the world's temptation and filth, where he might forget and be forgotten." However, the rules of existing religious orders were too stringent for his individualistic tastes. In 1894 he had written to a wealthy friend in Paris, outlining plans for a Strindbergian convent. The aim of the new order was to be "the education of man to superman through ascetic meditation, and the practice of science, religion and art." He was never particularly interested in religious aspects, "for one did not know what the religion of the future would be, or whether it would possess one at all."

Strindberg resisted all his friends' suggestions, deciding to atone in his own renegade fashion. Becoming an independent mystic was good for his work. The world always hungers for religious mystics who seem to provide an evanescent certainty lacking in the more stolid scientif-ically minded. Later Strindberg saw himself as a sage who transcended the restrictions of orthodox religions. In the "Blue Books" (1907-1908) he preached as a religious teacher, mixing mysticism with the remnants of his delusions so skillfully that many critics took his pronouncements seriously.

How would he perform the good works necessary for redemption? First, Strindberg thought that a quick way to cleanse his guilt would be to live in the midst of sufferings. In Biblical times he would have descended into the Valley of the Lepers—now he thought of a position as an attendant in a Parisian hospital. The idea soon faded in favor of a better method. A description of the horrors of insanity would serve as atonement by providing a penitent example to others. No longer would he corrupt Swedish youth with his writings—he would exorcise his illness by describing the sufferings that were the wages of sin. "The Inferno" ends with the admonition, "Such then is my life; a sign, an example to serve for the betterment of others; a proverb to set forth the nothingness of fame and of celebrity; a proverb to show the younger generation how they should not live."

Strindberg had passed through psychotic experiences for which many people possess the potential. He viewed them somewhat differently, because he was Strindberg. He was able to describe them more skillfully than other schizophrenics because he had a passion for understanding and a relentless drive for self-dissection, and because he remained more intact during these personality-shattering experiences. People who have been insane can understand the feelings of their brethren far better than those who use empathetic inference.

Although the dead can never return, the insane do, to give us a glimpse of the turmoil and tragedy of mental illness.

CHAPTER SEVEN

STRUGGLE *for* RECOVERY

When a person survives terrible experiences, they often become precious to him. They serve to raise him above the society of insensitive people to an attitude of ethereal disdain. If this applies to many ordinary occurrences, small wonder that it was true of the grandiosely-inclined Strindberg during his recovery from acute psychosis.

"Legends" starts where "The Inferno" ends, and describes the dying embers of his acute illness. In many ways it is not as valuable a description of schizophrenic feelings. There are indications in "Legends" that Strindberg, as he recovered, began to read books on psychology, which tended to distort the portrayal of his illness. For example, he speaks of a friend as showing "all the signs of hysteria described in Charcot's treatise." In the past he always had had a fleeting interest in psychology, without ever using contemporary psychological allusions in his literary work. However, one facet of his illness prevented this renewed preoccupation from having an adverse effect on his autobiographical writing. He never compares himself to psychological prototypes—with his grandiose feelings he believed that such mundane descriptions applied to common mortals, whereas it would require an intuitive genius to understand and describe the complexities of a Strindberg.

Unfortunately, he was having a very difficult time understanding himself. Strindberg felt as if he had two natures which were at war with each other. One part of his personality remained private; the other served as the image presented to the world for social purposes. Strindberg wrote, "I split up my personality, and show to the world a rationalistic occultist, but I keep my innermost individuality unimpaired and cherish the germ of a creedless religion—my two natures become so intricately intermixed that I can laugh at my newly won beliefs." Attempts to unravel these "two natures" ended in confusion and futility.

There were so many imponderables: Rediscovery of alcohol helps restore his conviviality, enabling him to establish closer relationships with people. Yet, although the period of extreme social withdrawal is over, he still feels that most men are inherently malicious, and that "the powers" are the only ones he can trust. Signs persist that he may become the prophet of a new era; strange noises indicate that nature is holding a special type of communication with him.

Strindberg continued to placate "the powers," maintaining the naive belief that attention to virtue would bring the reward of peace. Despite his sincere efforts to be a good penitent, the persecutions did not stop. Although they were present on a reduced scale, they were still annoying. An insect plagues him at night, and Strindberg is fascinated by its dance of death in the fire of the lamp. Upstairs neighbors make noise to persecute him. Any mysterious sound in the environment he refers to himself. A lifelong sense of injustice continues to torture him, in sickness as in health. Strindberg no longer protests, because, he says, "never once in my life have I succeeded in obtaining justice . . . Being born and predestined to suffer injustice, I have ceased to complain."

Masochism, the ability to experience pleasure out of pain, may be a blessing, serving as a defense against anxiety and the wish for death. This is one of the most striking things learned from the first section of "Legends." Since any attempt to battle the powers seemed to intensify the tortures of insanity, Strindberg decided to submit to all punishments. He would endure all of his torment in silence, as he had borne his punishment as a child. Indeed, he derived great pleasure out of suffering—"I swallow them down with a kind of grim joy in order to get done with them."

This strange universal characteristic has been seen in varying degrees and aspects, ranging from descriptions of martyrs dying in oblivious ecstasy, to less violent examples seen in psychiatric patients. In health, masochism seems like a perversion of normal functioning, but in mental illness it may act as a defense against additional deterioration. When Freud found a tendency of many patients to find pleasure in their remaining painful symptoms, he became disillusioned, thinking that this set up a barrier beyond which treatment could not progress. We feel that there was little reason for his dismay—he only encountered a necessary preserving defense in his patients. Freud always had to divide psychic life into opposites. Although he was a perceptive observer of mental functioning, it was one of his personal misfortunes never to have achieved the balanced wisdom and psychological understanding of Goethe. Goethe realized that what seems evil may at the same time be serving the good. Thus, guilt, while it often causes great suffering, also encourages good works and can be a preventive against further suffering. In the miracle play "Advent," written during his recovery period, Strindberg shows how guilt produces the expiation which can lead to forgiveness.

Possessed of new humility and resignation, Strindberg

feels that the experimental period of his life is over. His flirtation with science, instead of retaining faith in religious certainty, has yielded negative results. In the past he had been a seducer of youth. Now, with the aid of "the powers," he would become a prophet, to uplift his fellow intellectuals from stagnation, to present them with gods "intoxicated with the joys of life."

Did this apparent submission mean that he would cease seeking explanations for and the causes of his illness? This was one quest Strindberg could never abandon—he found himself much too interesting. First, there were the external aspects of his difficulties. What were the nature and origins of "the powers"? Here, Strindberg felt, one must tread softly, investigating in secret to avoid angering these august forces. His experiences in Sweden had demonstrated that "the powers" affected not only Dante, Swedenborg, and Strindberg, but lesser mortals as well. They were constantly operative and could change the structure and appearance of the world. When people attributed events to chance, they were unable to read the language of "the powers"; Strindberg attempted to decipher the system of symbols "the powers" used to proclaim their presence.

Then we come to the inner facets of his turmoil. Recovering schizophrenics characteristically pass their illnesses in review with varying degrees of depth. Filled with new hopes, Strindberg seeks to understand old fears. One of these fears was agoraphobia. This fear of open places was present for many years, during the acute psychotic illness, and became intimately connected with his paranoid feelings of persecution. He writes, "The aspect of the deserted marketplace makes a very painful impression on me, so that I desire to make myself invisible in order to escape curious eyes." Strindberg is now able to understand that this phobia is related to a fear of communication with others—he has to avoid open places for fear that he will meet other people who will expect him to converse with them. In order to walk in open spaces without succumbing to overwhelming anxiety and finally panic, he must blot out his surroundings—"I lower my head, fasten my eyes on the pavement, and feel as though I had compressed myself within myself, closed my senses, cut off communication with the outer world, and ceased to feel the influence of my surroundings." Phobias are so universal that their importance in schizophrenic illness has never been adequately defined. Strindberg's perceptive description suggests that phobias present in the previous personality may become connected with feelings of persecution and fear of communication during an acute schizophrenic illness.

Fear of communication with others became so intense that Strindberg looked for a method of dematerializing himself. At one time he was seized with the feeling that he could make his physiognomy change in appearance, and thought that he might be able to render himself invisible. Strindberg's phobia thus seems to have developed into feelings of depersonalization and derealization. This strongly suggests that schizophrenic feelings of unreality may be derivatives of previous phobias.

Another of Strindberg's major preoccupations was a consideration of the origin of the persecutory delusions themselves. Did they arise from within his person or come from outside? In "Legends," Strindberg answers this question as part of an essay titled "Observations on the Irradiation and Dilatability of the Soul." His analysis of feelings of persecution is in accord with modern psychiatric theory, approaching a complete understanding of the process of projection. Projection is the attributing of our own unacceptable feelings to others. Strindberg tells us that an individual can project parts of his personality outside of himself. For example, the paranoid individual has become over-sensitive to the feelings of others. Strindberg felt that he had become hypersensitive by the process of "exteriorization of sensibility." Ten years later in the "Blue Book," he amplified this perception using a fascinating analogy. "I happened once, when watching a spider in a web, to see her 'exteriorize her sensibility,' or in other words reel out a nerve-substance for herself with which she remains in touch, and by means of which she becomes aware when flies come and when the weather changes . . . Now it seems as though I had myself in a similar manner exteriorized my sensibility. I feel at a distance when anyone interferes with my destiny, when enemies threaten my personal existence, and also when people speak well of me or wish me well. I feel in the street whether those I meet are friends or foes . . . This makes life painful but rich and interesting." Strindberg recognized as externalized parts of his own personality the antennae which recorded the signals of potential enemies. Here the search stopped with the statement, "There are also projections which I cannot explain. It is possible that only poets and artists possess the power so to project their inward images in every life that they become half real."

Writing some years before Freud's discoveries, Strindberg appreciated the significance of dreams. In "Legends" he tells us, "For many years I have taken notes of all my dreams, and have arrived at the conviction that man leads a double life, that imaginations, fancies and dreams possess a kind of reality. So that we are all of us spiritual somnambulists, and in dreams commit acts which, according to their varying character, accompany us when we are awake with feelings of satisfaction or an evil conscience, and fears of the consequences." In "Alone" Strindberg said, "In dreams my innermost feelings are reflected, and therefore I can use them as I do my mirror while shaving." In "A Dream Play" he used dreams as dramatic material, trying to capture the essence of the dream world on the stage. Dreams were "disconnected but apparently logical," in them "time and space do not exist," and "the characters are split double and multiply; they evaporate, crystallize, scatter and converge." Strindberg became so fascinated with the importance of dreams that he related his feelings of persecution to dreaming life—"I believe that the so called persecution-mania really springs from the pains of conscience after evil deeds which one has committed in sleep, and of which vague recollections haunt us."

Swedenborg had a series of dreams at the beginning of his schizophrenic illness which he wrote down and later published. Strindberg now encountered these dreams of his redeemer, which he found identical with his own. His dreams like Swedenborg's were prophetic, promising him retribution when he was about to do evil, serving as instruments of "the powers," punishing him whenever he probed the secrets of nature and ceased to believe in God. Swedenborg had been the pilot who guided him between the Scylla of egotism and the Charybdis of false humility. However, as Strindberg improved, he began to have mixed feelings about his redeemer. Saviors also have ulterior motives—perhaps he had been rescued from one madhouse to be delivered into another. Swedenborg had been his Virgil, conducting him through Hell where he had seen all the evils he had committed since childhood. Now that the trip had been completed, Strindberg felt ready to overthrow his Savior, saying, "I have apologized for my culpable actions and I abjure my past."

Perhaps he would not be saved. There was so much to

regret, and judging from the misfortunes that had befallen his critics, bad times might come to the just and unjust alike. His past life had been "a network of crimes, a skein composed of godlessness, wickedness, blunders, brutalities." The fate of the sybarite in Mozart's *Don Giovanni* provided a fearsome prospect. Strindberg was frightened—"Fear of the unknown makes a man who thought he had solved the riddle of the Sphinx tremble." Now his Apologia began in earnest. This was the period during which Strindberg wrote "The Inferno" as part of his atonement. He pleaded that some of his early follies be forgiven, promising continuous atonement for his sins.

The gnawing fear that he might not be saved, coupled with one or more transient attacks of acute psychosis, revived the religious struggle and almost drove Strindberg into the Catholic Church. After completing "The Inferno," he journeyed to Paris to revisit his old acquaintances. Renewal of his scientific studies, this time more spiritual than chemical, caused a return of strange noises and compression in his chest. "I understand the hint. It is forbidden to penetrate into the secrets of the powers," he tells us. But where should he find a haven? One Sunday he wanders into Notre Dame to see the solemn grandeur of the Vespers. He visits other Catholic churches where "something rare, beautiful and wonderful is taking place there in the distance, amid the gold ornaments, incense, smoke and light." He touches the holy water and makes the sign of the Cross, stealing away into the night before being noticed. It was the everlasting maternalism of the Church, ready to forgive all transgressions, that attracted Strindberg so deeply, as it has attracted so many others laden with sin and despairing of forgiveness. After a frightening dream he speaks of it as the "Mother Church," telling what salvation means to him—"Since that night

I feel still more homeless than before in this world, and like a tired weary child, I long to be able to 'go home,' to rest my heavy head on a mother's bosom, to sleep on the lap of a mother, the pure spouse of an infinite God, who calls himself my Father, and whom I dare not approach."

But Strindberg's own mother had not been a Catholic, and his attraction to the Church departed. Besides, the Catholic type of penance failed to satisfy his craving. At his advanced age he couldn't possibly change his habits, not even for the sake of penitence. One particular aspect of the Catholic conception of Christ troubled his disordered mind. The Church said that Christ endured the ultimate in suffering for others. Strindberg replies, "He has certainly not suffered for us—for if He had, our sufferings would have been diminished." Strindberg never became a Catholic because his guilt could not be assuaged by Christ. He himself had suffered, and must continue to suffer, saying, "The Cross is for me the symbol of sufferings patiently borne, and not the token that Christ has suffered in my stead, for I must do that myself."

Theology was not really important, since all religions, including Swedenborg's, placed a high value on good works as a requirement for salvation. The purpose of religion was to provide "a quiet accompaniment to the monotonous music of life," Strindberg believed. He had disliked professional religion even before becoming ill. He extolled the Middle Ages, "when people knew how to enjoy and how to suffer.'" Yet suffering was non-sectarian, and inner righteousness was more important than prattling the liturgy. Job, persecuted by his family and friends, had possessed the true faith.

In the last section of "Legends," titled "Wrestling Jacob," after a Delacroix painting, Strindberg attempts a symbolic description of his religious struggles. The battles have sapped his energies, and he feels he is in the autumn of his life. Atavisms of the past return to quicken his discontent. Seeing a medal of himself, struck off when he had triumphed in the Stockholm trial after attacking the doctrine of Holy Communion, he is reminded of another sacrilege committed when he was fifteen. Memories of his Godless past create despair. Strindberg feels so unworthy that he says, "I am astonished that anyone has ever been able to love me."

Out of these depths of loneliness came a gradual realization of why he had needed religion so desperately. Religion had served as an antidote to emptiness. Now that the schizophrenic withdrawal has lessened, Strindberg finds loneliness oppressive rather than a blessing. He scoffs at his previous idea of entering a monastery—he has already lived like a monk too long. Contact with people, not parchments, is necessary—"As soon as I withdraw myself from the world, I am attacked by the evil spirit of madness," he says. So great now is his craving for companionship that he frequents bad company. Although not as paranoid, Strindberg is still too hypersensitive to be ready for normal interpersonal relationships. He knows that he has suffered from an illness, yet retains the tendency to blame outside forces—"Notwithstanding that I know its nature and significance, I am compelled to seek the cause of it outside myself." In this sentence is summarized one of the tragedies of the recovered schizophrenic. Even if he realizes that he has been ill, and that his persecutors have been unacceptable parts of himself which he has attempted to blot out, he continues to believe that the cause of the illness resides outside himself, in the world that still seems suspiciously hostile.

Strindberg felt that he had passed through unusual experiences which transcended the boundaries of logic. The persecutions in the last analysis had to be real. While he would not care to suffer them again, he treasures their memory. Unlike Dante and Swedenborg, who sent their friends and enemies to Hell during their own ascension to Heaven, he had gone through Hell and Purgatory himself. The purpose of the struggle seemed clear—"Sorrows are not punishments but tests." Strindberg is convinced that through suffering he has passed these tests, succeeding in establishing a link to God that will assure his salvation. With paeons to atonement he resolves to celebrate the victory. His creative talent returned, he would write plays to tell the world some of the sorrows he had known.

CHAPTER EIGHT

CALM *after the* STORM

Serenity and unproductivity need not be synonymous, but artists at peace with themselves are often sterile and dull. With many recovered schizophrenics the stream of productivity runs dry after an episode of mental illness; they survive, functioning at reduced capabilities, residua of illness preventing them from resuming a steady exploitation of their talents. Their work becomes stereotyped, obsessionally repeating the same themes, just as they had been preoccupied with delusions during their emotional turmoil.

Perhaps it is fortunate that Strindberg never fully recovered. Then he might have written in a monotonous style, and his later religious plays would have been suitable for church socials rather than the stage. Faith can be inspiring, but it can also impose incapacitating limitations. Strindberg never found solace in Christian absolutes, and his vagrant, uncontrolled feelings continued to fire his imagination. Still restless and unsatisfied, he had yearnings beyond his limitations which drove him on to new periods of stress. Illness had enervated his personality far less than it does those who have less energy to start with. Now that the afflictions had subsided and the disordered thoughts departed, Strindberg again had a feeling of triumphant self-confidence in his work.

This does not mean that the devastating illness failed to exert a profound effect on the rest of his life and work. It did. First, his psychotic experiences had widened his sensitivity to human feelings. He now knew about guilt in all its Satanic depths, and he became more cautious. As a young man Strindberg had started his career in a state of restlessness, without time to be wise or careful. Covetous of rapid success, he had offended others and the "gods." His poetic gifts had driven him unmercifully, more as a scourge than a blessing. Freda Uhl's sister had written, "He is so full of talent that he doesn't know what to do with it. But his is not a joyful way of creating. It is more like the savage impulse driving a murderer to his crime." Submission to morality had a mitigating effect, governing his talents and helping to conserve his energies.

With the exorcising of his demoniac qualities there came difficulty in writing. In the past creating had been effortless, and Strindberg had produced a succession of works in all literary forms with fantastic speed. Transmitting these new perceptions and feelings required different techniques. Reviving his career while residing in Lund, Strindberg established a working routine he was to adhere to for the rest of his life. Plays began appearing at regular intervals from late 1897, beginning with the first part of "The Road to Damascus." These later plays lack the trenchancy of "The Father" and "Miss Julie," but this is not their major fault. Strindberg's passion for unity had been fragmented by his illness, a condition no attempts at organization could rectify. The plays written during developing paranoia were brutally convincing because not one word was wasted. Whereas the early works were taut, the later plays became meandering. The repetitive theme of atonement is not what detracts from their effectiveness. The loosening of associations and forgetting of the dra-

matic unities scattered his ideas. Strindberg could write
brilliant isolated scenes, but the thinking disorder persisted to disturb the Gestalt, preventing him from weaving
the scenes into a coherent whole.

Although the residua of illness hampered the execution
of his writing, the insights gained through suffering deepened Strindberg's understanding of psychological motivations. As Schiller had been the trusted companion of his
developmental years, he now looked to the mature wisdom
of Goethe. Goethe once said that all of his writings were
fragments of a great confession, an idea which naturally
appealed to Strindberg. He envied Goethe, who appeared
to thrive on insecurity, passing through crises with a god-
like strength. Goethe possessed an Olympian calmness, a
harmony which Strindberg fantasied as concealing an
inner religious struggle. At last he saw that Goethe and
Schiller, far from being antagonists, supplemented and infused each other's experiences. In "Advent," one of the
first plays written after his recovery, Strindberg used
Faustian themes, writing, "I was an evil person and my
punishment is to serve the Good." Almost paraphrasing
Goethe, Strindberg said, "What's unborn is always most
beautiful. What's unwon, most dear."

Unfortunately, although Strindberg understood the
message of Goethe in his art, he could never use it in his
life. Falling in love with young girls was one of old
Goethe's practices, but Goethe had no illusions of regen-
erating himself. For Goethe the consummation of life had
more to do with the production of poetry than of children; the sight of an ancient lover reliving carnal desires
to escape loneliness and decrepitude was a little silly to
him. Not so with Strindberg. He may have said that a
man was a fool if he thought he could reproduce himself
in his own image, but he never stopped trying. During

his illness Strindberg had abandoned all hope of ever finding a woman with enough maternal compassion to take
care of him. Now his own person ceased to be important—
it was his progeny who were destined to serve the higher
purpose ordained by "the powers." With this belief, he
looked around for a nubile young girl to inseminate.

He found her playing Puck in *A Midsummer Night's
Dream* in Stockholm. It was a role calculated to revive
childhood fantasies. She was a twenty-two-year-old Norwegian actress named Harriet Bosse, lithe, ethereal, and
possessed of great beauty and talent. Strindberg wasted no
time, asking her if she would like to have his child long
before he proposed. This time he was under no illusions
that he had found a maternal woman; he knew that she
was ambitious like the others, and wanted to use his writing talents. Again his Pygmalion instincts were aroused;
in return for her bearing a child, he promised to write
plays for her and mold her into a great actress. Harriet,
like Freda, had Messianic zeal—maybe she could succeed
where the others had failed. The care and handling of the
famous Strindberg was always a fascinating adventure,
even if it ended in despair.

Whether making gold or attempting to make over a
woman, Strindberg was intolerant and disagreeable in his
perpetual search for dependency. Harriet Bosse was an in-
dividualist who maintained her independence and drove
Strindberg into a fury. For brief intervals the union was
idyllic, and this new female companionship had a salutary
influence on his work. Conjugal happiness inspired a return to mystical plays. Since writing "Lucky Peter's Journey," Strindberg had made the acquaintance of Maeter-
linck, the celebrated author of "The Bluebird," who
further stimulated his taste for the evanescent. Maeter-
linck's influence is very apparent in "Swanwhite" and

"The Crown Bride," two fantasy plays written as vehicles for his young Norwegian wife. Another unfortunate family tragedy catalyzed the creation of one of his most effective female characters. When Strindberg had tottered, Nietzsche had become insane; now as Strindberg was recovering, his sister had been committed to an asylum as a schizophrenic. Elizabeth Strindberg was eight years younger than he and had always been distant and strange. Yet she possessed a tenderness, a sense of other-worldliness that excited compassion and admiration. Since Strindberg believed that the world was a place of penance and tests, he began to feel that Elizabeth had been chosen to suffer for his sins, and in some measure for all of the world's sins. Strindberg had never attempted to empathize with the feelings of a female schizophrenic. Now, out of gratitude for her suffering, he eulogized his unfortunate sister as Eleonora in the play "Easter." Easter was a time of suffering as well as resurrection; the flowering of spring, as well as faith, had the power to soothe pain. Strindberg portrayed the female schizophrenic as having a heightened sensitivity to the beauties of nature, appreciating existence without concern about necessity and callous differences between right and wrong. Only the schizophrenic who had lost all concept of time and space could truly understand the meaning of life. Just as Siri had played herself in "Miss Julie" and "The Father," Strindberg saw Harriet Bosse triumph in the part of his psychotic sister in "Easter." Despite this stage success, Harriet found it increasingly difficult to tolerate his emotional instability. Seeing her drifting away, Strindberg quickly impregnated her, and as always there followed a period of tranquillity.

The essence of Strindberg's feelings following the recovery from his schizophrenic illness may be derived from three main sources. First, and most closely connected with the recovery phase, is the miracle play "The Road to Damascus," written in 1897-1901. The leading Swedish authority on this period of his life noted that the play-wright was still terrified by hallucinations and persecutory delusions when the first section was composed. For fuller comprehension of what Strindberg's mental processes were like during these later years, we must consult his prose works. In 1903 as his third wife was preparing to leave him, he wrote a short autobiographical book, "Einsam" (Alone), and in 1907-09 he produced a series of "Blue Books," using the same prophetic style Nietzsche had used in *Zarathustra*. All of these works recapitulate similar subject matter, and show Strindberg's relentless drive toward full realization of the psychodynamics of his illness and the method of recovery.

The first section of "The Road to Damascus" was written in Paris as Strindberg gradually returned to sanity; the second and third parts were composed in Sweden. The drama is a chronicle of his sufferings in the form of a modern morality play. "There is no such thing as happiness, only the strength to bear your destiny," he tells us at the outset. Strindberg covers the same period he delineated in "The Inferno" and "Legends," but now psychotic content is mingled with memories of his first marriage and the onset of his illness. Such productions are typical of the recovering schizophrenic—the events of panic become diluted with less frightening images of the past. The play contains a kaleidoscopic description of his feelings during developing paranoia, acute illness, and recovery. Disorganization prevents it from being dramatically effective, but does not detract from its importance as a psychological document. All the suspicions, ideas of influence, misogyny, grandiosity, penance, are mixed together with only the theme of a journey toward the Cross as a unifier. It is a

dramatic post mortem to explain why he had lost his
sanity. But as in most post mortems, the actual cause is
not revealed. Part of the play's purpose is to convince
others of the mystical reality of the strange experiences he
had passed through, transmitting what his psychosis had
taught him about human feelings.

Strindberg assumes the identity of a "Stranger." The
play begins in Berlin with his meeting a woman called
the "Lady"; this woman combines characteristics of his
first and second wives, and in the last part turns into his
mother. Woman's purpose is to lend him faith and save
him by her altruistic love, reconciling him to belief in
God. Strindberg here enlarges on previous conceptions of
his mother. He worships her ideal and rails against her
actuality, dividing her image into good and bad segments.
In the first section the Stranger tells the Lady, "I shall give
you a good character; your voice reminds me of my
mother—I mean the idea of a mother, for my mother
never caressed me, though I can remember her striking
me . . . That was the voice that first drew you to me, it
was like a mother speaking to her child."

Through the curious character of the Lady, representing an enigmatic blend of his two wives and his mother,
Strindberg develops his pathological ideas about women
still further. Wives and mothers were like Eve, to be worshipped before the fall from Paradise and despised when
they became temptresses. Eve "was a mother and brought
sin into the world. It was another mother who brought
expiation." The Lady, playing the good mother, attempts
to lead the Stranger into Church, but at first he feels in-
sufficiently cleansed, saying, "No, not into Church. It de-
presses me because I feel I don't belong there—that I'm
an unhappy soul, and that it's as impossible for me to
re-enter as to become a child again." Yet, he tries to excite

the Lady's maternal compassion and return to childhood. Even in childhood his life had seemed like a sentence. Judgment had been passed on him before he was born; he came into the world with guilt. "There are moments when I feel as if I have all the sin and sorrow, all the filth and shame of the whole world. I was born in disfavor, a step-child of life."

These romantic pronouncements demonstrate once again Strindberg's life-long sense of injustice and his desire for martyrdom. The Stranger continues, "When I grew older and wiser I saw that although the punishment wasn't earned I deserved it for other things that had never been discovered." Then comes a lauding of the pleasures of being beaten—"You see at every stroke of the lash I feel as if a debit entry had been erased from my ledger."

As the play progresses, Strindberg discovers two familiar reasons for his insanity. First, madness was a punishment for deciphering the secrets of nature—"If a mortal succeeds in penetrating the secrets of those above, no one believes him and he is struck with madness so that no one ever shall." The Stranger recognizes the connection between alchemy experiments and insanity when another character exclaims, "Does he want to make Gold? Is the man sane?" Secondly, guilt over stealing another man's wife can result in insanity. Marriage is sacred and immutable; the cuckold's soul is bound to the intruder, preventing him from building happiness on the sorrow of others. The Stranger steals the Lady away from her husband, just as Strindberg had done, and is hounded by the avenging husband, who says, "I shall come with a poppy, invisible to you, that will put your thoughts to sleep and confuse your mind, so that you'll see visions you can't distinguish from reality."

The characteristics of Strindberg's flight from reality

during the psychotic illness are graphically described in
"The Road to Damascus." First the feelings of grandiosity
—"I can survey the whole universe. I am the universe.
And I feel the power of the Creator within me, for I am
He." He speaks of being "under the ban of mysterious
powers who permit no mortals to interfere with their
work of vengeance." Then, feelings that his thoughts are
being read—"Who is it reads my secret thoughts, turns my
soul inside out and pursues me? Why do you persecute
me?" Finally, ideas of influence—the Stranger tells of a
man who went insane "through reading the works of a
certain writer whose notoriety is greater than his fame."

Those who are to be saved must repress hostility and
self-love. As he approaches his own Damascus, Strindberg
feels humble, having expressed his anger through the
making of gold. With poetic beauty he describes his
Shangri-La, a white monastery representing the home he
always wished for as a child—"I've never seen anything so
white on this polluted earth. At most only in my dreams!
Yes, that's my youthful dream of a house in which peace
and purity should dwell. A blessing on you, white house!
Now I've come home." Before he can ascend to the white
monastery, Strindberg meets with a Confessor, who tells
him, "Human greatness resides in the good opinion of
others." The sulphur fumes of the gold process have
served as part of his purification. Now he further purges
himself by abjuring his hatred of women, telling the Lady,
"I have made you evil, yet you're on the way to make me
good." The Lady shows him how the world has given him
maternal gifts he never acknowledged. Strindberg sees
this truth, and his guilt intensifies.

In the denouement of "The Road to Damascus," the
themes of religion and mother are united. The Lady informs the Stranger where the motive force needed to reach

the white monastery has come from. "By the strength of a mother's love—a mother's love—for so have I loved you, erring child, whom I've sought in the dark places of the wood, and whom at last I've found hungry and withered for want of love! Come back to me, prodigal one, and bury your tired head on my heart, where you rested before ever you saw the light of the sun." Then the Lady, who was his wife, changes into his mother, causing the Stranger to clamor in disbelief, "But my mother is dead!" He is told, "She was, but the dead aren't dead, and maternal love can conquer death." Women have been his strength and weakness, they caused his fall, yet provided for his redemption. Reaching the white monastery through the timeless love of his reincarnated mother, Strindberg is saved. With this reunion of religion and mother, "The Road to Damascus" ends.

Having resided in a psychotic world populated with less troublesome beings, the task of re-establishing contact with flesh and blood people, with all their demands and infirmities, was a difficult one for Strindberg. Actually, he never returned completely to reality. Having sampled the other world, he didn't particularly want to, and the remaining fragments of his illness prevented his full recovery. After Harriet Bosse left him, he ceased looking for reconciliation with mankind through a woman. In "Einsam" (Alone) Strindberg tells of the anguish suffered in becoming accustomed to a solitary existence, still battling against vestiges of the devastating "Inferno" years. Solitude was like "spinning oneself into the silken web of one's own soul, spinning a cocoon and waiting for the transformation." At first, isolation was accepted as a just punishment. Strindberg says, "I believe that it is my fate to be solitary, and that it is best for me." Loneliness seemed to have been forced upon him, and he invented many rationalizations to justify its continuation. In the state of solitude there was a free will lacking in the community, "an unheard of peace, a silent joy, a feeling of certainty and personal responsibility." There one was not a slave to necessity; there one could suffer in silence, adhering to a "confessionless Christianity." Living among people, in order to be sympathetic to human suffering, it was first necessary to arm yourself with brutality. Strindberg regretted his past hatred and lack of compassion for those he wounded.

While he was ill, comprehension of time seemed to have disappeared; now it had cruelly returned, and he was filled with remembrances and regrets. The sudden sense of advancing years was both painful and consoling. Maturity had taught him prudence in speaking and the nuances that made life more effective but less interesting. The elderly had memories but not enthusiasm; they were united not by common interests, but by virtue of increasing decrepitude. Although Strindberg could no longer join young revolutionary groups, it irked him when these organizations spoke of him as an old man. The old worried about propriety, asking questions just for the sake of inquiring. He possessed a silent envy of the young, who expended vast amounts of energy making new discoveries of old facts, filled with daring, unrestrained by constricting wisdom.

Strindberg made a poor adjustment to middle age, and had the additional misfortune to be plagued by the remnants of a devastating mental illness. Insights which his penetrating intelligence had derived from the past served more to frighten than to console. He reflects, "What happened in my childhood is so near in my recollection as if it happened last year . . . All the past was the litter in which the present grew. But the litter was burnt out, and without nourishment, and had begun to mildew." Suspiciousness continued to isolate him from people; he felt alone in groups and was particularly disturbed by the presence of women. Renewed antipathy toward women often separated him from potential friends. Now female destructiveness was diluted, seeming to upset his relationship to others rather than to be directed solely at him. Not that he coveted a stable home—married people were entangled in trivialities, lacked communication, and were "sentenced to loneliness at home."

How did Strindberg function, and what were his feelings while he existed in this solitary state? Although he certainly lacked the spirit of togetherness, no withdrawal similar to the schizophrenic panic occurred. When he felt unable to relate to others, he declared himself unwilling to accept companionship, and assumed an attitude of indifference. Yet he maintained an avid interest in environmental change, writing down everything he saw and heard. In the evenings he would meditate, hopeful of sinking into "the annihilation of sleep." Often, gazing in a hypnagogic trance at the walls and furniture of his rented room, he felt traces of love given to former occupants. This love was transmitted to him, resulting in a feeling of well-being. At the start of his schizophrenic illness we recall how he had wanted to abandon love. Now, after recovery, he absorbed it from any source, even inanimate objects endowed with distant memories of love given to others. As a young man he had required the approval of contemporaries. This craving for supportive relationships was still present. Strindberg now sat in street cars just to be among people. He was frightened lest people scorn him, fearful that in some way they had found out about his past psychotic hatred.

In this weird fashion Strindberg kept a controlled curiosity about humanity. From some he excited compassion and interest, as he had always been able to do. His solicitous landlady worried about his disorganized habits, and tried to give him emotional support, but he felt threatened by too intimate a relationship, and kept things impersonal. Long walks, which had always served as a prelude to creative activity, now fulfilled another function, that of establishing a speechless communication with regularly encountered strangers. There was a horseback rider he had known at the University thirty years before, an elderly lady walking her two dogs, a retired Major resigned to an imminent demise. Divining the human dramas behind these weary faces, and speculating on the conflicts lingering behind the flickering lights of the Stockholm homes, provided an endless game, and the street sounds, the noises emanating from neighbors' flats, which had once seemed like persecutions, now were blessed preservers of sanity. Someone plays Beethoven, the musical expression of a fellow sufferer, and Strindberg gratefully pauses to listen. Then he resumes his stroll on a route he has christened the "Via Dolorosa," filled with unfortunate reminiscences. He wants to forget the past, but it keeps intruding itself, leading to the conclusion that "As one is born, one remains pretty much unchanged throughout life." Reappraisals of former times had become futile, yet acceptance for one of his temperament was as painful as the struggle for understanding.

All during this period Strindberg fought a heroic battle against the almost incapacitating vestiges of his illness. First, there were the remaining feelings of grandiosity which became part of a vicious cycle. As his feelings of desolation increased, he became more grandiose to compensate for the emptiness. Finally, he would say, "I dare to change the world order, to steer the destinies of nations, to declare war and overthrow dynasties." On these occasions he reverted to the delusion that through his mind the ultimate truth would be revealed to mankind. Sometimes the seasons seemed specially designed to mirror his moods. Then there was his power of mental telepathy, a frightening yet precious gift which enabled him to maintain contact with absent friends and adversely influence his enemies. Some people seemed to be his born enemies; perhaps, through his telepathic powers, he had unwittingly interfered in their lives. Fortunately he believed that he could tell at a glance which stranger was an enemy and which one was a friend. Aging brought one major consolation—before, most of his enemies were ahead of him, now they had been pushed behind. Strindberg entered the final five years of his life still feeling persecuted, but filled with hope.

The "Blue Books" are the final sources of information to be mentioned, summarizing Strindberg's feelings as he approached death. They are volumes of pithy paragraphs, written in the form of a wise teacher preaching to a less enlightened pupil. The style was copied from Nietzsche's *Thus Spake Zarathustra,* but the content is not nearly as poetic or effective, and the intent is completely different. Strindberg's purpose is to convince others of the shallowness of materialism and the wisdom of the religious life. He has sampled all religions, Eastern and Western; although empathizing with the sufferings of Christ as embodied best in Catholicism, he has found all of them insufficient. Now the derivatives of schizophrenic grandiosity undergo a new transformation. During the acute psychosis, he had the feeling that "the powers" had planned some mysterious higher destiny for him. While recovering in Lund, he had felt that the world was an-

ticipating a miraculous religious revival. Although Strindberg never announced himself as a new prophet, there is
ample evidence in the "Blue Books" that he wished his
contemporaries to have a "Bible" of the religious principles he had discovered during his own sufferings. While
his dogmas were not as profound as Christianity, with
characteristic grandiosity he felt that they were just as
universal. Actually he was more unique than Christ—he
had survived! Christ wasn't around to talk to others after
the Crucifixion—he had to rely on disciples. Strindberg,
not being filled with love, had few disciples; but he had
his pen, a potent weapon for a semi-militant religious
revival. While not quite proclaiming Strindbergism, he
felt himself the hope of the non-sectarian.

There were some precedents for this. In the preface to
the "Blue Books" Strindberg writes, "I had read how
Goethe had once intended to write a Breviarium Univer-
sale, a book of edification for the adherents of all religions
. . . I felt myself constrained by inward impulses to write
a fairly unsectarian breviary; a word of wisdom for each
day in the year." The "Blue Book," besides covering religious subjects, includes a mélange of the brilliant psychological insights we have come to expect from Strindberg.
Derivatives of the illness were now present in a different,
socially acceptable form. Learning to live with psychotic
remnants required a barrier to filter out disturbing
stimuli. Strindberg describes how he insulated himself
against painful external sensations—"I have succeeded in
fabricating a kind of diving-costume, with which I protect
myself in society. When the insulting word or biting al-
lusion is uttered, the sound eventually reaches my ears,
but the receptive apparatus refuses to let it go further. In
the same way I can make myself literally blind. I obliter-
ate the face of the person I dislike. How it is done I do
not know, but it seems to be a psychological process."

Former delusions had mellowed with the passage of time. For example, the electrical persecuting machine was now an accumulator of faith—"The electric battery is Faith, which is not merely credence, but an apparatus for receiving and arousing the divine electricity—as it may be dangerous for an unbeliever to approach too near an accumulator. The faith-batteries of others can produce an effect on them, and they may be killed thereby, if they possess not the earth-circuit to carry off coarser earthly elements." Feelings of persecution were converted into a sense of unworthiness. Strindberg identified himself with Barabbas, the thief released before Christ was crucified. Like Barabbas, he had been "acquitted because of insufficient evidence" at the Stockholm blasphemy trial; subsequent experiences convinced him that "each carries his own heaven and hell within him."

Mild hatred of women and ideas of influence persisted in the "Blue Books." Strindberg wrote, "Man loves and woman hates; man gives and woman takes; man sacrifices, and woman devours." His hostilities still seemed to have a magical and frightening power—"One can hate and worry a man dead," he says. Both of these vestiges combined to make the legacy of his illness real and precious to him. "He who suffers from persecution mania is persecuted . . . Most of my misfortunes have been imaginary, but they have had the same effect as real ones, because I came to the consciousness of my wrongdoing." Guilt derived from suffering could become a blessing, resulting in a credo which subtly combined the spiritual and temporal. Strindberg ends the "Blue Books" with the admonition, "Pray, but work; suffer, but hope; keeping both the earth and the stars in view . . . Seek truth, for it is to be found, but only in one place, with Him who Himself is the Way, the Truth, and the Life."

Strindberg continued to work almost to the end of his

life, writing in the same confessional vein. Deep religious conviction did not prevent him from being furious when the Nobel Prize Committee ignored his work, honoring a less deserving countryman instead. There was one consolation. As a man grows older, the applause becomes more important, and the applause for Strindberg grew louder and louder. Social reform was sweeping over Sweden, and the aged playwright was hailed as its prophet. In the afternoons people read newspaper articles on the new movement written by Strindberg, tracing its origins to the abortive attempts in which he had participated. In the evenings the same people enjoyed performances of "Lucky Peter's Journey" and "Swanwhite," escaping into a fantasyland where all the mysogynistic plays were forgotten.

Respect and the affection of others convinced Strindberg that the years of atonement since his acute psychotic illness had been worthwhile. He had returned home and all his transgressions had been forgiven. Even the pain of stomach cancer was assuaged by an enormous display of popular esteem as he lay dying. The Stockholm *Aftonbladet* of May 15, 1912, describes his death: "He made a sign that he wished to have his Bible, which lay on the table by the bed. They gave it to him—he took it in his hand and said, 'All that is personal is now obliterated. I have done with life and closed the account. This is the only truth.' He kept the Bible clasped to his breast as he died."

CHAPTER NINE

METHOD *in his* MADNESS

Strindberg, caught in the maelstrom of mental illness, ranks first among all writers in need and ability to use his sufferings as subject matter for creative productions. The Collected Works of Strindberg fill fifty-five large volumes, nearly all of which are intensely autobiographical. He wrote incessantly, with boundless energy and an insatiable curiosity for research. To consider all of his published work is not fruitful, since Strindberg is repetitious and variable in creative powers, as is the case with nearly all other writers. We have already examined his main works of importance to psychology and the modern drama. Here we will stress other writings, where Strindberg's mental difficulties are displayed with unusual prominence. Many of these lesser works confirm what has been said, and some provide additional description of feelings during the development and decline of his mental symptoms.

Religious preoccupations not only color Strindberg's later plays, they were present from the beginning of his literary career. The spiritual struggles of his youth were intimately bound to grief at the death of his mother, and difficulties in adjustment to his stepmother. His earlier religious ideal was a saintly, misunderstood martyr, standing alone and stalwart in a rather adolescent battle against

society. Such an ideal is portrayed in "The Freethinker,"
one of his first attempts at playwriting. Strindberg's hero
passes through a spiritual crisis while seeking to revive the
basic principles of religious life. Leading his fellow youths
in a revolt against tradition, he is made a martyr by the
people who fail to understand his aims. Then, abandoned
by his loved ones, he becomes an ostracized wayfarer,
forced to leave the country which failed to appreciate his
prophetic soul.

In "The Freethinker," Strindberg succeeded in con-
fessing his own feelings and fears but failed to create an
artistic production. For his next attempt he decided it
would be in better taste to use historical characters as
oracles for his views. The Swedish Reformation was
chosen as the period, and well-known personalities like
Olaus Petri and the King Gustav Vasa became Strindbergian apologists. Strindberg was candid about his purposes, writing, "Back of the historical characters the
author would conceal himself, and in Olaus Petri he
would appear as the idealist, in Gustav Vasa as the realist."
The play was titled "Master Olof," and it became his
favorite literary creation, going through enough revisions
to delight generations of scholars. When it failed to gain
recognition written as a prose piece, Strindberg composed
a version in epic verse. After years of frustration, he finally
saw "Master Olof" produced and accepted as a contribution to Swedish culture. The Swedes continue to revere
this play for reasons it is difficult for a foreigner to comprehend. Perhaps beneath the frigid Lutheranism of modern
Sweden lurks religious unrest similar to the Reformation
upheaval. Master Olof was the militant preacher who aided
King Gustav Vasa in his battles with the Pope, incurring
excommunication by the Catholic Church. Olof's familial
and religious conflicts are identical with Strindberg's

doubts and fears. While his mother exhorts him to return to the old faith, Olof revels in his role as a heretic. Finally, caught in a conspiracy against the King who has been his paternal guide and protector, he is sentenced to death, saving himself by a last-minute recantation in the main Stockholm church. The play is very melodramatic and unconvincing, except as a further indication of the intensity of Strindberg's passionate struggles.

Strindberg next tried to tackle his religious problems at the summit, writing the first draft of a play on the ordeals of Christ, "Jesus of Nazareth." Since he was not yet possessed of grandiose feelings, Strindberg felt incapable of doing justice to such a sublime subject, and the project was abandoned. But he was already obsessed with doubts about his own sanity, causing him to begin writing a historical play about the psychotic Swedish King Erik XIV, which he failed to complete. Later, after his acute schizophrenic illness, he did succeed in writing a drama describing this regal fellow sufferer.

Strindberg continually used religious themes, changing their emphasis as his personal experience widened and his illness deepened. The creative process itself seemed like a mystical religious experience to him. He felt in a state of Nirvana while writing, lapsing into a twilight sleep of pleasant exhaustion after finishing a play. Following his marriage to Siri Von Essen, religion became mingled with woman and love, and the scene of battle was shifted to cathedrals and convents. In "The Secret of the Guild," conflict rages during the building of the Cathedral of Uppsala, where love and marriage conquer all adversity, and the hero is vindicated through the faithful support of a woman. As his paranoia developed, Strindberg wrote dramas for Siri to play herself on the stage, gazing with fascinated horror from the wings while she

subtly destroyed her own image. Such a play was "Sir
Bengt's Marriage," where the religious theme persisted in
the opening scenes. The heroine, a Nun Margit, marries
a knight when the nunneries are closed, then discovers
that marriage, like religious dedication, can become an
exhausting affair. Siri played Margit as Strindberg dissected his grievances against women in general and his
wife in particular. The play ends happily with the penitent wife admitting that man is master, a denouement
Strindberg devoutly wished would occur at home. The
tempestuous relationship between the knight and his lady
foreshadowed the turmoil described in "The Confession
of a Fool."

On rare occasions Strindberg tried to separate his creative work from his illness by writing mystical plays, but
even here the psychopathology was blatantly evident.
"Lucky Peter's Journey" has been accepted as a fairy tale
with a Peter Pan-like quality despite its plaintive theme
of redemption through a woman. In the world of elves
and leprechauns, marriages were made in Heaven, even
though Strindberg's own marriage seemed like Hell on
earth. The hero Peter is told by the fairy Lisa, "Mark you,
when a little baby boy is born into the world, a little baby
girl is also born somewhere; and they seek and seek until
they find each other. Sometimes they go amiss as to the
right one, then it turns out badly; sometimes they never
find each other, then there is much sorrow and affliction;
but when they find each other, then there is joy, and it is
the greatest joy that life holds."

When his marital difficulties and persecutory ideas increased, Strindberg could no longer dilute his feelings
with such saccharine. Ibsen and the craze for female emancipation provided the inspiration for the next series of
plays. We have already noted how Strindberg included

Ibsen personally in his developing delusions, accusing Ibsen of using his marital strife as subject material for the drama "The Wild Duck." Now the stage became an outlet for his suspicions, a cathartic arena used to forestall further mental disintegration. "The Comrades" is a minor play written at the same time as "The Confession of a Fool." Marital strife is the theme, but the wife just enervates the creative husband like a vampire sucking blood, stealing his productivity and passing it off as her own. Woman is a thief, not a persecutor; she weakens man, but does not seek his destruction. "The Father" was Strindberg's next play. Here woman weakens man for the purpose of making him mad.

Thus the progress of Strindberg's illness can be followed from play to play, as he derived masochistic pleasure from watching the horrible spectacle of his sickness unfold on the stage. The cycle continued with "Creditors," overshadowed by the brilliance of "The Father" but nonetheless highly esteemed in France. Again female machinations are the main subject. The wife, Tekla, acted by Siri Von Essen, induces her former husband to drive her second husband, Adolph, insane. Adolph, tortured like Strindberg by guilt over stealing another man's wife, accepts his fate with resignation. He has sinned, and allowing the cuckold's revenge is part of his atonement. This motif passed into the "Inferno" period, to become an integral part of the playwright's psychotic illness.

Strindberg continued to use his personal life and misfortunes for dramatic material long after the separation from Siri and the notorious divorce. The divorce itself was dramatized in "The Link," a play dominated by a preoccupation with his children's fate. Children were the links of even a loveless marriage. The Baron tells his wife of the bond their son has become. "He is the memory of our beautiful hours, the link that unites our souls, the common ground where we must ever meet without wishing to do so."

Remorse over the desertion of his growing children became the theme of another series of works. Mothers could destroy as well as create; only men could feel altruistic maternal love. In the grotesque "Mother Love," a mother's possessiveness devours an adolescent girl, preventing her from developing to maturity. "The Key of Heaven" tells of a sorrowful man who has lost his most precious possessions, his children. As already mentioned, the poem "Laokoon" pictures a mysogynist supplicating mercy before God for his children, offering to sacrifice himself. In "Facing Death" the sacrifice is carried out, as a father destroys himself to redeem his unfaithful children.

Although artistic production ceased during Strindberg's acute schizophrenic illness, the occult scientific writings that were composed revealed a persisting method in his madness. The most fascinating book written during this period was "Antibarbarus," dealing with theories of chemical elements. Motivated by an insane hatred of the world, Strindberg nevertheless hit upon the idea of transmutation of basic chemical substances, at the same time as the Curies were beginning their experimentation with radium. When Strindberg proclaimed that sulphur was not an element, he was wrong; but when he postulated that many of the substances scientists called elements were made up of hydrogen atoms, and that higher elements could be broken down into lower ones, he was anticipating epochal discoveries of modern physics. These scientific theories went unnoticed because they were pure speculations, lacking experimental proof. Yet, their brilliance again testifies to his genius, in sickness as in health.

After his recovery, Strindberg sought in vain to rid him-

self of the impact of Siri Von Essen. Neither of his other
wives had any lasting significance, while Siri's image appears again and again in different costume in his later
plays. Previously, in a drama aptly titled "Playing with
Fire," he had presented the triangular affair from which
he had emerged as the successful lover. In "There Are
Crimes and Crimes," psychotic ideas of influence were
added to the plot. Siri is portrayed as Henriette, a
coquette who seduces the famous playwright Maurice.
When their illicit embraces are disturbed by the thought
of Maurice's child, the couple wish the child dead. The
wish is fulfilled; the child dies, just as Siri's child had
died of pneumonia while she consummated the original
liaison with Strindberg. In addition, Maurice has stolen
Henriette from his best friend, betraying a trust just as
Strindberg had done twenty-five years before when ab-
sconding with Siri. The couple are suspected of murder,
and even acquittal does not assuage their guilt. Maurice
learns that humans must assume responsibility for their
thoughts and desires, as well as for their deeds. Evil intentions are punishable by conscience. "There are crimes not
mentioned in the Criminal Code, and these are the worse
ones, for they have to be punished by ourselves, and no
judge could be more severe than we are against ourselves."

Thus the husband-wife conflict was resuscitated in
Strindberg's work, with a new variation. Eroding guilt
and retribution, residua of schizophrenic illness, now in-
filtrated the battle of the sexes. "The Dance of Death"
was written just prior to his third marriage, and is the
post-illness version of "The Father." Husband and wife
again decapitate each other in scene after scene, spewing
venomous hatred at all who cross their path. The wife,
Alice, is no longer pictured as evil incarnate because
Strindberg is haunted by his own contribution to Siri's

misery. This time the Captain is more malicious than his mate; he is the aggressor, plotting her downfall, retaliating thrust for thrust. Destructiveness no longer originates in a "motiveless malignancy"—it is a result of emptiness in life. Both partners are aging victims of an ennui which has weakened their vitality rather than tempering their glowering hatred for each other. In a macabre scene, Alice plays a melody, "The Entry of the Boyars," enticing her husband into a frenzied dance that causes a fainting brief encounter with death. As the play ends, the Captain dies, saying, "Forgive them, for they know not what they do." No one was to blame, Strindberg now believed. People were destined to persecute one another, and atone for sins they were not responsible for. Death brought a serene peace, "wonderful as the solemn anxiety that surrounds the coming of a child into the world." Writing on the eve of his third marriage, Strindberg infused the second act with a note of hope in his portrayal of a young couple on the threshold of matrimony. Although "it is the unmistakable right of every human being to suffer misfortune," even fifty-two-year-old misogynists had a duty to pursue elusive happiness.

Momentary contentment with his third wife and the prospect of another child brought a return to the mystical in "Swanwhite" and "A Dream Play." Here Strindberg created two of his most popular plays, the public tending to ignore the psychopathology while enjoying the fairy-tale atmosphere. In "Swanwhite" he resurrected the image of his mother, that long-suffering woman he had so thoroughly vilified in the autobiographies. Watching his pregnant wife, he decided that mothers could never be really evil; those who appeared to be evil were merely enchanted. Swanwhite's mother is magically called back from the realm of death and made pure.

However, after Harriet Bosse left him, maternal stock dipped to a new low. Mothers were never safe with Strindberg—his portrayal of their virtues and vices depended on immediate supplies of female support. In "The Pelican" the mother is a vicious creature who devours her young while complaining about the offsprings' ingratitude. Her son tells her, "Do you know why I am so sick? I have not had the maternal breast, but have been bottle-fed by a servant." Later the angry young man says, "A son speaking to his mother like this is doing something contrary to nature, but some things must be said." Strindberg said them, loud and often. In "A Dream Play" he tried to recreate the world of the dream, but the drama became a mélange of Zen Buddhism and Strindbergian torment. It is another "Road" play, similar to the harrowing trip to Damascus; his dream characters have shifting identities, representing condensations of his wives and other significant people. Familiar themes are dissected—unjust punishment, pangs of conscience, stealing another man's wife (punishable by insanity), redemption through a woman. Small wonder that Strindberg's declining years were plagued by insomnia.

During his last creative period Strindberg was preoccupied with visual effects and experimented with new stage techniques in a series of chamber plays. Only one of these works has endured—"The Ghost Sonata." Remnants of the psychotic illness are still strongly in evidence here, and the eerie qualities of this play are not entirely due to innovations of staging. Ideas of influence, powers of mental telepathy, people dematerializing into the invisible—all of this makes one suspect that the author has suffered a recurrence of his sickness. However, the recovery veneer is also present. Retribution is the principal motif. Each dramatic character has skeletons in his closet and must suffer punishment for past sins. Strindberg always presented the whole truth, a practice which made him very unpopular. In his last play, "The Great Highway," he compared himself to the eternal wanderer and Biblical truthseeker, Ishmael. Writing partly in prose and partly in unrhymed iambic verse, he leads us on another two-hour journey through his miserable past, an unrewarding trip completely devoid of dramatic conflict. But, even when ineffective, he provides some interesting touches, like the facetious comment on Christian good works: "There is more joy in giving than receiving, but to be robbed is no fun." Then there is his suggestion that people suspected of being sane are the ones who should be kept under surveillance. Finally, Strindberg speculates that those who become mad experience less suffering, and expresses regret that he had not completely lost his sanity. When "The Great Highway" received a poor reception, Strindberg ceased writing, feeling that his few remaining conflicts should be kept personal.

Strindberg also wrote a cycle of twenty-three historical dramas detailing every period of Swedish history. There were many motivations for this return to the historical format. During the recovery process, he disguised his continuing grandiosity by identifying himself with people of noble birth. When the urgency of the "Inferno" period had been replaced by resignation, Strindberg accepted the obvious fact that others had faced similar perturbation. Describing the psychic misfortunes of well known historical figures required less personal involvement than he displayed in "The Father" and "Miss Julie." But, since mental difficulties were universal and timeless, he could easily insert the familiar themes. The historical plays also represent part of his atonement to the Swedish people. In his realistic plays Strindberg had ridiculed family life and had been accused of corrupting Swedish youth. Now he redeemed himself by publicizing Swedish history, and presenting slightly tarnished heroes to the young.

The cycle was started in Lund during his recovery, beginning with a portrayal of the earliest Swedish Kings in "The Saga of the Folkungs." King Magnus, like the recovering Strindberg, had been falsely maligned and was forced to bear the sins of others in addition to his own. Again, the theme was guilt and punishment; the punishment was insanity followed by an interminable atonement. Hovering over the incipient phases of Swedish royalty Strindberg saw the same Powers as those which seemed to be controlling his own destiny.

The next historical play represented a continuation of his first Herculean effort, "Master Olof." For psychological purposes, "Gustav Vasa" is of more interest for the delineation of the king's son than of Gustav himself. This son was the unfortunate Erik, the future psychotic King Erik XIV. Twenty-five years before, Strindberg had burned the first draft of a play about Erik. Now, having passed through schizophrenic experiences himself, he felt ready to complete the tragedy. "Gustav Vasa" continues the story of the Swedish monarchy twenty years after the time of "Master Olof," with Strindberg making an appearance as the tottering Erik, the disdained heir apparent. The already paranoid Erik complains of his heritage, saying, "My blood was poisoned at birth." Like Strindberg, Erik displays his ambivalent conflict in a quarrel with his stepmother—"You must not be in love with your stepmother, and yet you must love her! that's madness too." Erik expresses the author's feelings when he tells his stepmother, "My heart lies buried in my mother's coffin in the vaults of Uppsala Cathedral." In the companion play "Erik XIV," the young king becomes more agitated, finally going mad with suspicion as he tries unsuccessfully to atone for inherited guilt. Life must be a punishment for guilt—a motif that occurs again and again in Strindberg's later plays.

Queen Christina was the only woman who ever occupied the Swedish throne, having ascended at the age of six after her famous father, Gustavus Adolphus, had been killed during the Thirty Years War. She was a fascinating, enigmatic young woman, a veritable museum of psychopathology who shared many of Strindberg's conflicts and interests. Although she was a serious student who invited Descartes and other European intellectuals to Stockholm, she possessed a quixotic temperament, making her unsuited to bear regal responsibility. Tormented by religious and sexual struggles, she finally abdicated at twenty-eight to become a Catholic and make a pilgrimage to Rome. Strangely enough, Strindberg, in his play "Queen Christina," dwells only briefly on the religious conflict, presenting the Queen as a woman who tried unsuccessfully to fill a masculine role. Caught in a tragic revolt against female biology, Christina indulges in coquettish love affairs, flirtations during which deep affection changes mercurially into hatred. Christina's attempt to compete with men turns her into an androgynous creature, hating both women and men, a fate similar to that suffered by Miss Julie.

The most famous Swedish kings were not noted for their stable psychological adjustments. Charles XII, known to his contemporaries and posterity as the "Madman of the North," was a mother's boy like Strindberg. His dislike of female companionship became legendary, and was not conducive to Swedish succession. To many of his subjects this deficiency of libido was a relief. Charles ruined Sweden, and provided an example to Napoleon and all future conquerors of Russia by his debacle at Poltava. In the play "Charles XII," Strindberg emphasized the psychic conflict of the defeated warrior king during the last three years of his life. Charles is controlled by the Powers, those ubiquitous forces so distressing to Strindberg. The Powers had ordained the king's destruction. Since he was unable and unwilling to do penance, he remained doomed. Charles was a stubborn gambler who showed no concern for loss of human life. Yet, Strindberg tells us, he loved his mother—"The only woman I have ever loved because she was my mother, and so . . . was not a woman to me." Once again, Strindberg wove his personal conflicts into an historical narrative.

Gustav III, assassinated at the Masked Ball immortalized by Verdi, was the most artistically sensitive of the Swedish kings. Strindberg's play "Gustav III" isolates selected facets of the king's personality of greatest interest to the dramatist. Gustav was an actor and author, producing plays in a palace theatre and skillfully using histrionics in his regal duties. He excited patriotic displays by dressing in native costumes and making flamboyant appearances among his subjects. After one of the King's escapades a character comments, "The exit was not quite as happy as the entrance. But that happens even to the best of actors." This flair for theatricalism in public was not the only thing Gustav had in common with Strindberg. The King had many problems with women, which contemporary scandal attributed to impotence. He also possessed many effeminate characterstics, and a homosexual conflict is intimated in the play. Gustav began to believe gossip and, like Strindberg, came to doubt the paternity of his children. This doubt eventually led, not to insanity but to reckless self-exposure, terminating in a tragic death.

When the subject was madness, Strindberg always made the most of it. From historical epics to marital discord, from fairy tales to macabre death, he ranged in a grandiose and often pathetic display of his suffering. At first, recognition was the object of his artistic creativity. Fame was achieved, followed by notoriety as his dramas became part of a relentless vendetta against female emancipation and his imagined persecutors. Then a hiatus, when he fled in schizophrenic panic, withdrawing from the world, once so fascinating but now seemingly filled with hatred. Finally salvation, obsessed with guilt, writing plays of atonement describing his religious recovery. As an artist, Strindberg was blessed with every talent except a sense of humor. The only pleasure he experienced came from a communion with nature or a distillation of his personal suffering. Laughter, he lacked; he lived a cheerless life, reproaching himself for imagined sins while providing his perceptions for the enlightenment of others.

CHAPTER TEN

WISDOM *from* AFFLICTION

Those who minister to diseased minds have been impeded by lack of knowledge of the feelings of the mentally ill. Unfortunately, the majority of schizophrenics can tell us little about their affliction. Sympathetic hospital aides have extracted some understanding of schizophrenic feelings after years of subtle interpersonal contact, first fending off hostility, later achieving a type of mutual trust. This trust is non-verbal, and the knowledge likewise is incapable of being transmitted to others. In a desperate attempt at bridging this gap, psychiatrists have advised their students to descend into the psychotic world while remaining anchored in sanity.

Mental illness, to the average schizophrenic, becomes a private affair, to be guarded against intruders. The paranoid individual may be vociferous about his persecutory ideas, but such outbursts contribute little information about his personal feelings. Yet, as Strindberg said in "The Road to Damascus," "Madmen are in reality the only wise men, for they can see, hear and feel the invisible, the inaudible and the intangible, though they cannot relate their experiences to others." Thus the revelations of schizophrenics with poetic insight like Strindberg assume extreme importance.

Extrapolating from one case to many is a difficult and

deceiving task, but many clues toward understanding the
symptoms and distorted feelings of the schizophrenic may
be derived from the perceptions left by Strindberg. His
self descriptions verify many previously held theories, and
add a great amount of new information. First, the genetic
constitutional factors in schizophrenic illness are sup-
ported by the Strindberg case history. He had a younger
sister who spent most of her life as a chronic schizophrenic
in a mental hospital. Feeling a close kinship with this
unfortunate girl, Strindberg came to believe that she had
been punished as part of the atonement for his sins.
Many of his previous misdeeds were attributed to a constitutional sense of injustice that plagued him all his life.
Future paranoid individuals seem to share this predispo-
sition, leading them in the direction of serious difficulty
as they progress into adulthood. Strindberg recognized
that the symptom complexes of his disturbance did not
arise by chance, but represented coalescing aspects of his
former personality. This realization caused him to stress
early mother-child relationships as being of crucial importance in later mental illness, thereby anticipating modern emphasis on the neglectful "schizophrenogenic"
mother. He blamed his own mother for lack of attention
and for creating a type of Madonna-worship that resulted in the choice of unsuitable wives who triggered off
his suspicions. The vistas of childhood provided further
evidence of the continuity between illness and health in
his fascination with electricity and chemistry. Scientific
interests provided the basis for his delusion of being
persecuted by an electrical machine, while they acted as
preservers of sanity. This innate fascination with the
mechanisms of the external world was part of a personality endowment outwardly free from constriction. Knowledge of science and the Gestalt aided his recovery, en-

abling him to question the reality of his persecutions. Also, his constitutionally passionate nature served to combat an acquired tendency to introspection, helping further in his struggle to resist the scourges of devastating illness.

The consummate hatred shown by many schizophrenics is demonstrated again in Strindberg's case in a fascinating way. One of Strindberg's delusions was that he had succeeded in manufacturing gold from the baser elements. Penetrating the secrets of alchemy was the means of venting his tremendous hostility on the world. Making gold would destroy the traditional order by upsetting the balance of trade, and the psychotic playwright fantasied himself surveying the economic ruin like a conqueror viewing the remnants of a razed city. Long before the acute illness, Strindberg possessed an unexcelled awareness of the extent of his anger; he warned his first wife during their courtship to "Beware of the sick Lion. Don't come near his den or he will kill you with his caresses." This perception that his anger at times reached psychotic proportions motivated a search for its origins, which deepened his self-understanding. Current psychological theory claims that recovery from mental illness depends on the capacity for insight. Strindberg's case verifies this concept. His incessant self-analysis prior to acute illness seems to have prevented a more serious attack and facilitated recovery.

Strindberg's autobiographical description also shows how schizophrenic illness can be successfully postponed or even avoided by a favorable environmental constellation. Despite his impaired capacity for interpersonal contact, the schizophrenic desperately needs people. Tormented by tremendous hostility, he manipulates his environment, testing the sincerity of proffered friendship, enticing others to persecute him. When the people who surround him respond with the failings of ordinary mortals, he withdraws, seeking refuge in the self-adulation that protects him from total destruction. Strindberg's friends never deserted him despite continual testing and personal attacks. While he failed to excite all of the compassion he required, he nevertheless inspired enough interest to prevent a lapse into chronic illness. Inborn suspicions always remained with him, but paranoid ideas were mollified whenever he was mothered, symptoms waxing and waning with the supplies of supportive care.

This inordinate need for mothering was linked to severe disturbances in Strindberg's sexual life. He had an even more pronounced difficulty in viewing his parents as sexual beings than that shown by ordinary people. As is the case with many schizophrenics, he was prevented from reaching a mature heterosexual adjustment by a streak of ascetic puritanism. Strong evidence of homosexual conflict was evident in the development of his delusions. Fighting against acceptance of these sexual conflicts, he acted them out in his dramas and in his marriages. This demonstrates again that the schizophrenic, far from being quietly introspective, is constantly displaying his turmoil in a variety of ways. Strindberg's sexual difficulties drove him to steal another man's wife, incorrectly fantasying this woman as the reincarnated mother who would save him. When that marriage failed, the anticipated savior became a persecutor, calling down upon him the revenge of the husband he had wronged. When his marital life ceased to provide a sufficient outlet, Strindberg used his creative work as a catharsis for sexual and other conflicts. His illness and the debacle of his first marriage were used as source material for all of his later writings.

The schizophrenic's constant drive toward mental

health is graphically illustrated by the events of Strindberg's acute illness. He repeatedly tested the reality of
his distorted perceptions in a steady effort to regain his
sanity. The incident when the hallucinating playwright
took a compass to bed with him, to test scientifically for
the presence of an electric current he felt was being
passed through his body, is one of the most amazing
examples of reality testing ever recorded. This need to
question disturbed thoughts also thrust him toward other
people both sane and demented. Thus the mentally ill
Nietzsche, suffering from similar psychotic preoccupations,
gave Strindberg needed support at a crucial period of his
creative life. Rediscovery of his brilliant schizophrenic
countryman Swedenborg added dimension to his atonement, providing him with the faith needed to continue
his interrupted career as a writer.

Strindberg's illness exacted a greater toll from his personality than from his literary gifts. Remnants of his
psychotic delusions were obvious to all of his contemporaries. He continued to fancy himself beset with enemies,
and felt powerful enough to exert evil influence on them
through mental telepathy. No matter how much insight he
developed, he still felt that the cause of his illness resided
outside of himself. His difficulty in associating with people
was related to a feeling of being above them, of having
experienced tortures that ordinary mortals could not comprehend. Even during recovery, Strindberg maintained
the psychotic belief that he had been destined for some
high purpose, and saw himself as a misunderstood Nietzschean Superman. Illness had hypertrophied his conscience, leaving him with an inhibiting sense of guilt
which precluded enjoyment of all pleasure. Trapped by
these remnants of painful yet precious experiences, Strindberg sought escape through rebirth fantasies, seeking to

create offspring who would inherit wisdom from his affliction along with fresh enthusiasm and confidence.

Strindberg's autobiographical writings contribute many
new glimpses into the psychotic world. Fortunately, his
fear of people did not extend to fellow sufferers from
mental illness or to potential audiences. Brilliant insane
people seem to possess a hunger for companionship, unlike ordinary schizophrenics who seldom seek to share
their experiences with others. So intense was Strindberg's
desire to have mankind participate in his misfortunes,
that even histrionic displays failed to dilute their significance.

One of the major memories of his boyhood was fear,
and his subtle dissection of childhood fears highlights the
importance of phobias in schizophrenic illness. Children
commonly have phobias which disappear during maturation. As he develops, the child gradually becomes more
gregarious. He assimilates the threatening environment
and ceases to fear being left alone. Strindberg's childhood phobias persisted into adult life, becoming linked
with the panic that occurred during his acute psychosis.
Describing a feeling of fright in open spaces, Strindberg
related his agoraphobia to fear of communication with
others. Slowly this feeling grew into a desire to dematerial-
ize, to make himself invisible, providing the ultimate defense against ominous intruders. Strindberg's poignant
description is strong evidence that schizophrenic feelings
of depersonalization and derealization are derivatives of
a fear of communication that is traceable to adult and
childhood phobias.

Strindberg's communication with the Almighty was
eased rather than obstructed by his schizophrenic illness.
Indeed, religion played a prominent part in his psychotic
symptomatology, as is usual in such episodes. We have

shown how the themes of religion and mother dominated the playwright's creative productions from the beginning. During recovery, Strindberg returned to the religious feelings and exhortations of his mother, seeking to unite himself with her adored image. Similarly, religion serves other schizophrenics as a socially acceptable framework in which to solve their conflicts. During the acute illness the schizophrenic feels that people hate him, and he detests them in return as he seeks to destroy his persecutors. Gradually, although still filled with rancor, he may come to look on himself as Christ-like. With further restitution there commences a search for a method of forgiveness. Empathy with Christ now becomes an effective medium through which previous hatred may be neutralized. Christ loved others despite their betrayal and persecution. He symbolizes the ultimate in forgiveness, the spirit of Christian resignation. The schizophrenic comes to view religious principles as a means of achieving salvation, which helps him to say truthfully, "I forgive them, for they know not what they do."

Religion was for Strindberg a potent method of assuaging schizophrenic hatred. Should religious preoccupations then be encouraged in other schizophrenics? Distorted feelings are more easily modified than disordered thoughts. Encouraging religious convictions when they appear may prove to be of greater value than attempting to persuade the schizophrenic to question the reality of his persecutors. Religion often represents a renaissance of deep yearnings derived from early years of personality development. In Strindberg's case it was a realization of the connection between past and present that determined his future recovery. Perhaps, through the area of religious compromise, others with less perceptual endowment can be similarly aided.

During the period of recovery Strindberg swung back

and forth between grandiosity and humility. Although he recognized the grandiosity as often concealing feelings of emptiness and fear, the attendant euphoria is described with such fervor that it becomes obvious how the recovered schizophrenic treasures his psychotic experiences, no matter how painful they have been. Lurking behind the recovering psychotic's humility is the belief that his illness has made him into a very special person. Although the schizophrenic constantly strives for recovery, this does not mean that he has failed to derive some satisfaction from his illness. It is hard for us to fathom how desolation can also contain gratification, yet Strindberg's revelations show that this is the case. Autobiographical descriptions of the playwright's suffering teach us a great deal about this fundamental protective mechanism built into human behavior. Strindberg always felt the need of punishment. As a child, his sense of injustice drove him to a constant search for martyrdom; when punishment was withheld, his symptoms worsened. This quest for martyrdom has been observed in many other schizophrenics in childhood. It may foster the illness by displaying to adults a desire to be persecuted. Perhaps it is derived from what psychoanalysts call "Oedipal guilt." Strindberg suffered from this type of guilt after stealing another man's wife. He blatantly described Siri Von Essen as a substitute mother, mistress of the very house his mother had presided over during his childhood. Insanity to him came to represent the result of a cuckold's revenge. Had this guilt been removed, it might have been impossible for him to have expiated his sins by a return to the religion of his mother.

Feelings of guilt are not always destructive, and may provide a means of respite. The universal characteristic of masochism, the ability to extract pleasure from pain, seems to act as a protective defense in schizophrenia, as it does in other forms of mental illness. This suggests that the schizophrenic requires affection tempered with realistic chastisement. Perhaps it is not only suspiciousness, but a concomitant need for punishment which causes him to question the love of others.

Knowledge of human feelings is cumulative, growing by insight and perseverance. The vast, continuous tragedy of mental suffering requires information from diverse sources. Many creative artists have suffered from insanity and have written of their feelings of precious desolation. Strindberg, whose perceptions enabled him to see deeper and further than his psychotic brethren, stands as a monument to human capacity with its ceaseless drive to comprehend.

CHAPTER ELEVEN

STRINDBERG *and* O'NEILL

This appended chapter presents some comments on Strindberg and the most celebrated twentieth-century American playwright, Eugene O'Neill. As we have already indicated in the Preface. O'Neill paid tribute to Strindberg's inspiration, particularly in his acceptance speech for the Nobel Prize, which Sweden had strangely failed to award to its own native genius. O'Neill also felt great empathy for the Swedes, who were given the first production rights to his posthumous plays.

Strindberg and O'Neill belong to separate generations and come from vastly different heritages. The initial connection between the two playwrights occurred as an aftermath of death. Strindberg died in May, 1912. The twenty-four-year-old O'Neill had just returned from his final ocean voyage to his favorite saloon, Jimmy the Priest's, where he resumed his alcoholic debauchery. The saloon had been the scene of a suicidal gesture two years before, during a depression triggered off by marital difficulties. The family now arranged a divorce and O'Neill was pressed into service in his father's stock company. They returned to New London, Connecticut, in August, to that eroding atmosphere described in *Long Day's Journey into Night*. O'Neill's mother was addicted to drugs, and his father and older brother drank heavily. Then Eugene fell ill with tuberculosis and entered Gaylord Sanitarium in December, 1912.

Meanwhile, an interesting phenomenon occurred in the publishing business. Despite Strindberg's fame in Europe, there had been no demand for English editions of his books. Suddenly, this changed. Eleven Strindberg works were translated into English in 1912, thirteen in 1913, and twenty-one in 1914. First editions were quickly sold out, and productions of his plays were announced in Chicago, New York, and Berkeley, Califorina. The only Strindberg play previously performed in the United States had been "Miss Julie," presented in Russian at the Thalia Theater, New York, in 1905.

Clayton Hamilton, a playwright and critic, made the ailing O'Neill aware of Strindberg's contribution to the drama and suggested a reading of the English translations of his plays. Strindberg, however, was not the only influence on O'Neill during this formative period of enforced idleness. O'Neill shared Strindberg's interest in Nietzsche's *Thus Spake Zarathustra,* in the writings of Schopenhauer, and in the necrophilic stories of Poe. He digested the Elizabethan classics, and was fascinated by the taut structure—and also the plagiaristic opportunities—present in the Greek tragedies.

O'Neill gradually synthesized a method of freeing himself from his sick family and triumphing over his father's mediocrity. Writing plays became a type of supportive therapy necessary for psychic survival. He went through his period of apprenticeship and imitation, reading passages from "Miss Julie" to all who would listen, trying to use Strindberg's short stories about marriage as source material for plays.

Unfortunately, O'Neill never fully understood Strindberg's contribution to modern drama. First, he had poor judgment as a critic and no awareness of Strindberg's psychotic illness. O'Neill began his career by writing one-act plays similar to Strindberg's shorter dramas. He experimented with the material he knew best, namely, his sea experiences and his emotional unrest. During this period he worshipped the Strindberg who had written "Miss Julie" and "The Father," trying to preserve unity of action and brevity of expression.

Then something happened. O'Neill lost interest in Strindberg's naturalistic dramas, and started to rave about the Swede's loosely-constructed plays like "The Dream Play" and "The Spook Sonata." Skeletons in the closet became more important than the people on the stage. He was a ruminator, haunted by family memories, tortured by conflicts he seemed too weak to solve. Writing was a catharsis, serving to postpone his inevitable fate.

At first O'Neill's pessimistic determinism did not affect his output. *The Long Voyage Home, Beyond the Horizon* and *The Emperor Jones* are brilliant plays, which contain none of the pontificating characteristic of his later productions. O'Neill's literary development was completely different from Strindberg's. The Swedish playwright reached his peak just before his psychotic illness, then survived to write plays of personal and historical atonement. Strindberg tried every artistic form, including novels, poetry, and painting. He was an unsuccessful actor, a struggling journalist, and a fugitive bohemian. He successfully translated his personal tragedy into stage characters that continue to serve as symbols of universal misery.

O'Neill, like Strindberg, wrote best when he wrote about himself, but he failed to mature and he became excessively introspective with increasing age. Fame brought with it an increase of appetite that devoured his early genius. Like James Joyce, he began to expect homage rather than attention. His plays became longer and longer, as if he enjoyed watching his audiences squirm in their seats for hours.

No artist grows great by engaging in self-justification. Strindberg and O'Neill both suffered from this failing. Strindberg, apologizing for stealing another man's wife, is just as ineffective as O'Neill dissecting his family like an anatomist. Neither matured like Shakespeare, who grew wiser and more perceptive with each play, his later plays ending as a testament of philosophic wisdom. The best of O'Neill lies in his poetic descriptions of his spiritual communion with the sea. The best of Strindberg lies in his coruscating attack on women and in his battle with madness.

Actually, their psychic difficulties were similar in content. Both Strindberg and O'Neill believed in mysticism and in ideas of influence. Both blamed parental mismanagement for their misfortunes, something that has become fashionable since Freud pointed an accusing finger at his own innocent father and mother. Both had psychiatric treatment, and both suffered from the lingering hostilities of that perpetual villain, the Oedipus complex. Both were dependent on women, had three marriages, and were unable to maintain satisfactory sexual adjustments.

This is where the similarity ends. Strindberg, ravaged by mental illness, remained robust and vigorous, while O'Neill became maudlin and pompous. Strindberg was a cosmopolite, with a deep appreciation of European culture and a continuous hunger for knowledge. O'Neill was a New England provincial, who lived his life like a Greek tragedy and expected his audience to form the chorus. While humility remained at the base of Strind-

berg's psychotic grandiosity, O'Neill placed ever-increas-
ing demands on actors and producers. He became as
arrogant as Wagner. Sitting through a performance of
Long Day's Journey into Night is like suffering through
a rendition of *Parsifal*—there is beautiful music, but, as
Nietzsche said, "It sweats."

Strindberg's dialogue is never labored like O'Neill's.
Even his later plays retain a sense of spontaneity, an effortless movement in the midst of anguish. He says what
has to be said without putting too much traffic on the
stage. O'Neill possessed this gift in the early plays, then
abandoned conciseness in favor of a grotesque, epic style.

O'Neill retained his ability to write scenes, but lost the
art of composing plays. Strindberg had taught him how to
use personal experience for psychological material, but
O'Neill corrupted the method. Perhaps his decline is
traceable to the cumulative effects of whiskey or the
tubercle bacilli that were eating away at his adrenals.
No one will ever know why the man who might have
become a twentieth-century Melville deteriorated into a
taproom philosopher.

The agonies Strindberg and O'Neill present on the
stage evoke totally different emotions from audiences.
One feels pity for Strindberg as he fights to discover the
origins of his difficulties. His characters battle desperately,
but they never beat themselves to death. The audience
leaves the theater thoughtful and alert, with a greater
realization of human complexity.

Popular reaction to a recent revival of *Strange Interlude* illustrated O'Neill's effect on an audience. Curtain
time was six P.M. A swinging sign at the adjoining restaurant advertised a "Special *Strange Interlude* Dinner" at
8:30 P.M. Here was an American classic, performed with
skilled dedication by a fine cast, the reviewers had said.
Lobby conversation revealed that most of the patrons

had come out of a sense of duty. Anyone seriously interested in the theatre had to attend. The play lasted
almost five hours, during which time several effeminate
men competed for the attention of a colorless, neurotic
woman. Except for occasional flashes of excitement and
O'Neill's frequent demonstration of verbal virtuosity, the
audience had no emotional involvement with the events
or the people on the stage. The drama seemed dated,
humorless, and dull.

When the one-hour intermission arrived, the audience
made a mad dash for food and drink to revive their
benumbed senses. Waiters at the nearby restaurant went
through gymnastics to get everyone served in the limited
span of time. One man was overheard saying, "This is
silly. Why didn't they all go to bed with her in the first
three acts so that we could go home and relax?"

It was a good question, which remained unanswered.
Everybody (except the wise few) ran back to their seats
as the warning buzzer sounded to announce the resump-
tion of the play. By eleven P.M. a large segment of the
audience was either yawning or asleep. The final curtain
calls were greeted with enthusiastic applause for the val-
iant cast who had almost succeeded in creating a mean-
ingful play out of the lifeless material.

Yet, O'Neill's plays are much more popular than
Strindberg's. Even in Sweden, the premiere of a new
O'Neill play is greeted as a national event. Why? The
Swedish psychology is easier to understand. O'Neill is
depressed and introspective. He possesses a Gothic mys-
tique. He is mournful, a fitting accompaniment to long
winter nights and days without sunshine. He reawakens
the lost spirit of the Vikings, of the days before the
Swedes had started to make their fortunes out of ball
bearings.

In America, O'Neill is riding the crest of a cult of

self-immolators similar to the Nietzsche enthusiasts of
the past. When people have a reservoir of senseless anger,
they will deify a writer who expresses their mood. The
later plays of O'Neill do this. O'Neill wanders like a
pathologist in a morgue, performing autopsies without
ever discovering the cause of death. He praises the quit-
ters and the outcasts and lays waste to the optimists.

Strindberg had a deeper perception. He saw that conflict was not purposeless and failure was not inevitable.
People battle with each other and with themselves for a
reason. Life is often sordid, but men look for hope in the
presence of decay. There is always a meaning in tragedy,
an enrichment distilled from sadness that helps a little,
even if it does not lead to complete salvation.

O'Neill could never have written without Strindberg,
but he did not inherit his sense of futility from the
Swedish genius. This feeling separates him from the psychological drama Strindberg inspired, and it damages his
plays. Strindberg wrote in the preface to "Miss Julie,"
"First of all, there is no absolute evil. That one family
perishes is the fortune of another family which thereby
gets a chance to rise. And the alternation of ascent and
descent constitutes one of life's main charms, as fortune
is solely determined by comparison."

Strindberg saw man in flux, never ceasing to evolve.
His characters retain their dignity while they fight their
guilts. O'Neill was a man of pessimistic temperament like
Schopenhauer. He believed in the impossibility of happiness and in the likelihood of nothingness. A world that
feels itself to be on the brink of extinction is bound to
appreciate him. It is doubtful if posterity will be so kind.

BIBLIOGRAPHY

BOOKS

ADAMOV, A. *August Strindberg—Dramaturge.* Paris, L'Arche, 1955.
AHLSTROM, STELLAN. *Strindbergs Erövring au Paris.* Stockholm, Almquist & Wiksell, 1956.
ARIETI, S. *Interpretation of Schizophrenia.* New York, Brunner, 1955.
BALZAC, H. *Seraphita and Other Stories.* Trans. C. Bell and R. Scott, New York, Burt, 1905.
BLEULER, E. *Dementia Praecox or the Group of Schizophrenias.* Trans. J. Zinkin, New York, Int. Universities Press, 1950.
BONAPARTE, MARIE. *The Life and Works of Edgar Allan Poe—A Psychoanalytic Interpretation.* London, Imago, 1949.
BRANDELL, G. *Strindberg's Inferno Kris.* Stockholm, A. Bonnier, 1950.
BREDSDORFF, E., MORTENSEN, B. AND POPPERWELL, R. *An Introduction to Scandinavian Literature.* Cambridge, Cambridge University Press, 1951.
BRINTON, C. *Nietzsche.* Cambridge, Harvard University Press, 1941.
CAMPBELL, G. A. *Strindberg* (Great Lives Series). London, Duckworth, 1933.
CLARK, B. *Eugene O'Neill—The Man and His Plays.* New York, Dover, 1947.
COMMAGER, HENRY S. *Theodore Parker.* Boston, Little, Brown & Co., 1936.
EKLUND, T. *Fran Fjärdingen Till Blatornet.* Stockholm, Bonnier, 1946.
———. *Tjänstekvinnans Son En Psykologisk Strindbergstudie.* Stockholm, A. Bonnier, 1948.
FÖRSTER-NIETZSCHE, E. *The Life of Nietzsche.* Trans. P. Cohn. New York, Sturgis & Walton, 1915.
FREUD, S. *Collected Papers,* Vols. 1-5. London, Hogarth Press, 1953.
FROMM-REICHMANN, F. *Psychoanalysis and Psychotherapy.* Selected Papers. Chicago, University Press, 1959.

GASSNER, J. *The Theatre in Our Times.* New York, Crown, 1954.

GOETHE, JOHANN. *Faust.* Trans. B. Taylor. New York, The Modern Library, 1950.

HELLER, OTTO. *Prophets of Dissent.* New York, Alfred A. Knopf, 1919.

HIRSCH, WILLIAM. *Genius and Degeneration, A Psychological Study.* New York, D. Appleton & Co., 1896.

HITSCHMANN, E. *Great Men: (Swedenborg).* Psychoanalytic Studies. New York, Int. Universities Press, 1955.

HOHLENBERG, JOHANNES. *Sören Kierkegaard.* New York, Pantheon, 1954.

IBSEN, H. *Brand—A Dramatic Poem.* London, Everyman-Dent, 1951.

JASPERS, KARL. *Strindberg und Van Gogh.* Bern, E. Bircher, 1922.

JOLIVET, A. *Le Theatre de Strindberg.* Paris, Boivin, 1931.

JONES, E. *The Life and Work of Sigmund Freud.* Vols. 1-3, New York, Basic Books, 1955.

JOSEPHSON, M. *Zola and His Time.* New York, Macaulay, 1928.

KAUFMANN, W. *Nietzsche—Philosopher, Psychologist, AntiChrist.* New York, Meridian, 1956.

KIERKEGAARD, S. *Either/Or: A Fragment of Life.* Trans. D. & L. Swenson. Princeton, University Press, 1944.

KRIS, E. *Psychoanalytic Explorations in Art.* New York, Int. Universities Press, 1952.

LANGE-EICHBAUM, W. *Genie, Irrsinn und Ruhm,* Fourth Edition. Munich, Reinhardt, 1956.

LIND-AF-HAGEBY. *August Strindberg, The Spirit of Revolt.* New York, D. Appleton & Co., 1913.

LUDWIG, E. *Goethe—The History of a Man.* New York, Putnam, 1928.

McGILL, V. J. *August Strindberg—The Bedeviled Viking.* London, Noel Doublas, 1930.

MORTENSEN, BRITA AND DOWNS, BRIAN W. *Strindberg—An Introduction to His Life and Work.* Cambridge, Cambridge University Press, 1949.

NIETZSCHE, FRIEDRICH. *Thus Spake Zarathustra.* New York, The Modern Library, 1956.

———. *The Philosophy of Nietzsche.* New York, Int. Universities Press, 1955.

NORMANN, D. *Strindbergs Skilmassa Fran Siri Von Essen.* Stockholm, Natur Och Kultur, 1953.

NOYES, A. *Modern Clinical Psychiatry,* Fourth Edition. Philadelphia, Saunders, 1954.

NUNBERG, H. *Principles of Psychoaanlysis.* New York, Int. Universities Press, 1955.

PODACH, E. *The Madness of Nietzsche.* Trans. F. Voigt. London, Putnam, 1931.

ROBERTSON, J. G. *Outlines of The History of German Literature.* London, Blackwood, 1950.

SCHILLER, J. C. F. *The Robbers,* Trans. H. Bohn. New York, Stringer & Townsend, 1850.

SCHLEICH, KARL L. *Hagkomster Om Strindberg.* Stockholm, Björck & Börjesson, 1917.

SCHREBER, D. P. *Memoirs of My Nervous Illness,* Trans. I. MacAlpine & R. Hunter. London, Wm. Dawson & Sons, 1955.

SIGSTEDT, C. *The Swedenborg Epic.* New York, Bookman Associates, 1952.

SMIRNOFF, KARIN. *Strindbergs Första Hustru.* Stockholm, A. Bonniers, 1926.

SPRIGGE, ELIZABETH. *The Strange Life of August Strindberg.* New York, The Macmillan Company, 1949.

STRECKER, K. *Nietzsche und Strindberg.* Munich, G. Müller, 1921.

STRINDBERG, AUGUST. *Advent.* Trans. Claud Field. Boston, Richard Badger, 1913.

———. *Cinq Pieces En Un Acte.* Paris, Delamain et Boutelleau, 1927.

———. *Creditors, Pariah.* Trans. E. Björkman. New York, Scribner's, 1912.

———. *Easter,* Trans. V. Howard. Cincinnati, Stewart & Kidd, 1913.

———. *Eight Famous Plays.* New York, Scribner's, 1949.

———. *Einsam (Alone).* Munich, Georg Müller, 1909.

———. *Fair Haven and Foul Strand.* New York, McBride, Nast & Company, 1914.

———. *Gustav Adolf,* Trans. W. Johnson. Seattle, University of Washington Press, 1957.

———. "Have Plants Nerves?" New York, The Tucker Publishing Co., 1900.

———. *Historical Miniatures,* Trans. Claud Field. London, George Allen & Company, 1913.

———. *Legends.* London, Andrew Melrose, 1912.

———. *Le Pelican.* Paris, Theatre Popularie, 1956.

———. *Lucky Pehr.* Trans. V. Howard. Cincinnati, Stewart & Kidd, 1912.

———. *Margit (La Femme du Chevalier Bengt).* Trans. Georges Loiseau. Paris, Soc. du Mercure de France, 1898.

———. *Married.* Trans. E. Schleussner. London, Palmer, 1915.

———. *Notice sur Les Relations de la Suede Avec La Chine et Les Pays Tartares Depuis le Milieu du XVI Siecle Jusqu'a Nos Jours.*

Paris, Libraire de l'Ecole du Louvre de la Societe Asiatique, De L'Ecole Des Langues, 1884.

———. *On The Seaboard.* Trans. E. Westergren. Cincinnati, Stewart & Kidd, 1913.

———. *Queen Christina, Charles XII, Gustav III.* Trans. Walter Johnson. Seattle, University of Washington Press, 1955.

———. *Six Plays of Strindberg.* Trans. E. Sprigge. New York, Doubleday Anchor, 1956.

———. *Swanwhite.* Philadelphia, Brown Brothers, 1909.

———. *The Confession of a Fool.* Trans. E. Schleussner. Boston, Small & Maynard, 1913.

———. *The Great Highway* (In *Modern Scandinavian Plays*). New York, The American Scandinavian Foundation, 1954.

———. *The Growth of a Soul.* Trans. Claud Field. London, William Rider & Son, Ltd., 1913.

———. *The Inferno.* Trans. Claud Field. New York, Putnam, 1913.

———. *The People of Hemsö.* Trans. E. Schubert. Stockholm, Bonniers, 1959.

———. *The Red Room.* Trans. E. Schleussner. New York, Putnam, 1913.

———. *The Road to Damascus.* Trans. G. Rawson. London, Jonathan Cape, 1939.

———. *The Saga of the Folkungs.* Trans. Walter Johnson. Seattle, University of Washington Press, 1959.

———. *The Son of a Servant.* Trans. Claud Field. London, William Rider & Son Ltd., 1913.

———. *The Vasa Trilogy; Master Olof, Gustavus Vasa, Erik XIV.* Trans. Walter Johnson. Seattle, University of Washington Press, 1959.

———. *Zones of the Spirit* ("Blue Book"). Trans. Claud Field. New York, Putnam, 1913.

STRINDBERG, FREDA. *Marriage with Genius.* London, Jonathan Cape, 1937.

SULLIVAN, HARRY S. *Clinical Studies in Psychiatry.* New York, Norton, 1956.

TOKSVIG, S. *Emanuel Swedenborg—Scientist and Mystic.* New Haven, Yale University Press, 1948.

UDDGREN, GUSTAF. *Strindberg the Man.* Trans. Axel Johan Uppvall. Boston, The Four Seas Co., 1920.

UPPVALL, AXEL J. *August Strindberg—A Psychoanalytic Study With Special Reference to the Oedipus Complex.* Boston, The Gorman Press (Richard Badger), 1920.

PAPERS

BACHLER, KARL. "August Strindberg—Eine Psychoanalytische Studie." *Internationaler Psychoanalytischer,* 11, 5, 1931.

BALINE, ALICE. *"Identification"*—in *The Yearbook of Psychoanalysis,* Vol. 1, New York, Int. Universities Press, 1945.

BJÖRKMAN, EDWIN. "August Strindberg—His Achievement." *Forum,* 47, 145, 1912.

BRETT, A. "Psychological Abnormalities in August Strindberg." *Journal of English and Germanic Philology,* 20, 47, 1921.

COLEMAN, STANLEY. "August Strindberg—the Autobiographies." *Psychoanalytic Review* 23, 1936.

DAHLSTRÖM, C. "August Strindberg—Between Two Eras." *Scandinavian Studies,* 21, 1, 1949.

FREUD, S. "Psychoanalytic Notes Upon an Autobiographical Account of a Case of Paranoia (Schreber Case)," *Collected Papers,* Vol. 3, p. 387. London, Hogarth Press, 1953.

FROSCH, JOHN. "Transference Derivatives of the Family Romance." *Journal of the American Psychoanalytic Association,* 7, 503, 1959.

GUSTAFSON, ALRIK. "Recent Developments and Future Prospects in Strindberg Studies. *Modern Philology,* 46, 1, 1948.

———. "Strindberg and Björnson in Paris." *Yearbook of The American Institute of Swedish Arts,* 1944, p. 53.

HAUGEN, EINAR. "Strindberg the Regenerated." *Journal of English and Germanic Philology,* 29, 257, 1930.

HAYWARD, IRA. "Strindberg's Influence on Eugene O'Neill." *Poet Lore,* 29, 596, 1928.

JOLIVET, A. "Strindberg et Nietzsche." *Revue de Literature Comparee,* 19, 39, 1939.

KLAF, F. & DAVIS, C. "Homosexuality and Paranoid Schizophrenia." *American Journal of Psychiatry,* 116, 1070, 1960.

KLAF, F. "Nietzsche's Poetic Insight into the Psychotic Process." *Psychoanalysis and The Psychoanalytic Review,* 6, 81, 1959.

LAGRIFFE, L. "La Psychologie d'Auguste Strindberg." *Journal de Psychologie,* 1912.

LIE, ERIK. "Strindberg's Suspicion." *The Living Age,* Vol. 3, 1921.

LIND-AF-HAGEBY, L. "August Strindberg—a Study Lecture Delivered Before The Anglo-Swedish Society, Dec. 6, 1927." London, A K Press, 1928.

NIETZSCHE, F. "Lettres Inedités de Frederic Nietzsche et August Strindberg." *Revue,* 101, 310, 1913.

O'NEILL, EUGENE. "Strindberg and Our Theatre" *in* Deutsch, Helen,

and Hannan, Stella, *The Provincetown, a Story of the Theatre,*
p. 191. New York, Farrar, Rinehart, Inc., New York, 1931.
————. "Proud of Debt to Strindberg." *American Swedish Monthly,*
31, 20, 1937.
RAPP, ESTHER. "Strindberg Bibliography." *Scandinavian Studies,* 23,
109, 1951.
ROMO, G. "Nietzsche, Precurseur de la Psychoanalyse." *Evolut.
Psychiat.,* 1, 55, 1935.
SCHEFFAUER, HERMAN. "A Correspondence Between Nietzsche and
Strindberg." *North American Review,* 198, 197, 1913.
SITWELL, OSBERT. "The Man Who Drove Strindberg Mad." *Life and
Letters To-day,* 28, 141, 1941.
Strindberg's Divorce Letters, Courtesy of Mr. Lennart Lofveblad,
Sandbergs Bok Handel, Sturegatan 8, Stockholm.
TAUSK, VICTOR. "On the Origin of the Influencing Machine in
Schizophrenia." *Psychoanalytic Quarterly,* 2, 1933.
UPPVALL, AXEL J. "Strindberg in the Light of Psychoanalysis." *Scan-
dinavian Studies,* 21, 133, 1949.
VOWLES, R. B. "Tennessee Williams and Strindberg." *Modern Drama,*
1, 166, 1958.

INDEX